The Eucharist in Four Dimensions

I read this lovely book and imagine I am standing at the four corners of an altar table, enjoying four lovely conversations. I am satisfied, but still hungry for more. This Eucharist, and these rich conversations are rations for my journey until I see Jesus face to face. This is a book to be ravished – and ravished by.

Stephen Cottrell, Archbishop of York

I sometimes forget why I first fell in love with Christianity. This book has helped me fall in love with it all over again. It is rooted, reparative and wise.

Ben Quash, Professor of Christianity & the Arts,
King's College London

Jessica Martin here offers a powerful inquiry that manages the unlikely feat of being at once deeply meditative and fizzingly provocative. Those who find the Eucharist a (or the) central Christian practice will here find diagnostic profundity – Where are we, in our sacramental lives, and how did we get here? – and imaginative hope – What promise of unexpected grace is held up before us? An essential book for our moment.

Alan Jacob, Professor of Humanities, Baylor University

Jessica Martin's book creates an entirely new genre: not liturgical theology, nor even sacramental theology in the traditional sense, but an exhilarating combination of profound theological scholarship, literary insight, and cultural commentary on what it is that we are about when we 'do this in memory' of Christ. A most thought-provoking and imaginative contribution to the post-pandemic discussion about the future of the Church and its life.

Sarah Coakley, University of Cambridge
and Australian Catholic University

What a gem of a book! It is rich and deep, thoughtful and stimulating. It is very much not the last word on everything you might want to know about the Eucharist, instead it reflects, suggests and tantalizes so that you discover more – more questions, more meaning, more depth. I really enjoyed it.

Paula Gooder, writer and lecturer in biblical studies

The Eucharist in Four Dimensions

The Meanings of Communion in Contemporary Culture

Jessica Martin

CANTERBURY
PRESS
Norwich

© Jessica Martin 2023

First published in 2023 by the Canterbury Press Norwich
Editorial office
3rd Floor, Invicta House
108–114 Golden Lane
London EC1Y OTG, UK

www.canterburypress.co.uk

Canterbury Press is an imprint of Hymns Ancient & Modern Ltd
(a registered charity)

Hymns Ancient & Modern® is a registered trademark of
Hymns Ancient & Modern Ltd
13A Hellesdon Park Road, Norwich,
Norfolk NR6 5DR, UK

British Library Cataloguing in Publication data

A catalogue record for this book is available
from the British Library

978 1-78622-472-9

Typeset by Regent Typesetting
Printed and bound in Great Britain by
CPI Group (UK) Ltd

Contents

When he was at the table with them, he took bread, blessed and broke it, and gave it to them. Then their eyes were opened, and they recognized him; and he vanished from their sight.

The Gospel of Luke, 24.30–31

[I]t was a garden where He was crucified. For though it has now been most highly adorned with royal gifts, yet formerly it was a garden, and the signs and remnants of this remain.

Cyril of Jerusalem, Catechetical Lectures, XIV,
'On the Words, "And Rose Again from the Dead
on the Third Day" …' para. 5

Introduction

This book began as a lecture series, the Bampton Lectures, which I gave at the University Church of St Mary the Virgin, Oxford, in May 2021. The world was cautiously opening up following the pandemic lockdown, so I gave two of the lectures (including the one on 'schemes and screens') to an empty church with a livestream camera. The final two had a small live audience, a quite different experience. Across the book there will be signs and remnants of its original pandemic context: those I have left in the text belong in the larger argument. I am enormously grateful to the selection committee for the Bampton Lectureship, to the University of Oxford, and to the kind welcome and hospitality of Will Lamb and Jane Shaw. All had a part in giving me the opportunity to explore this subject.

I had been thinking about it for a while – before the pandemic ever happened. The book you have in your hands is the second in a series of three, which each explore from different angles how the glorious Body of Christ coheres with the fragile, flawed gathering of human bodies struggling to live in that Body now. Our late modern cultural context is a difficult one for an incarnational faith. It is doubtful about the reality status of anything you can't handle or prove, yet it is also dominated by virtual engagement. And virtual engagement is itself an inconsistent kind of space. It is rich in the rhetoric of bodily affirmation, but at the same time it expects metaphysical convictions of identity to have limitless power. It's defined by individualist assertion, even though it's shaped by and subject to homogenizing marketization. And, while it is contemptuous of the collective demands of organized religion, it assiduously polices secular polarized ideologies. Finally, it defines desire as the highest human good, but is permeated with a consumerism that buys and sells people and their hopes.

I wrote about the effects of all this in my last book, *Holiness and Desire*, discussing how it has shaped both sides of the sexuality debate within the Church. And I will be looking at it again in a future book called *In the Body*, which will explore how the bodily metaphors that shape Church identity are both used and misused in order to maintain some kind of communal coherence against the backdrop of our unquestioning cultural belief in personal autonomy.

But *this* book is about the eucharist, the central encounter with Christ's Body at the heart of Christian hope. And it thinks not only about how the rite of eucharist can subsist in a world so apparently sceptical of sacred symbolic powers, but also at the part the historical arguments about what the eucharist is, and how it can happen, have played in spreading and establishing that very scepticism. So this is not the right book for you if you are looking for the detail of eucharistic liturgy, or a careful summary of its theoretical arguments in historical order. Those already exist. This is a book emerging out of what our doctrinal divisions on the eucharist have done to modern apprehensions of what is real. At the same time, it asks how the performative practice of eucharist might continue to have power in a culture so conditioned to be deaf to the Word. I consider the eucharist through metaphors of the four dimensions, three of space and one of time, so that the rite is understood throughout as an event in the world and not only as an idea.

Finally, as in *Holiness and Desire*, I have coped with this being far too big a subject for a small book (or even a large one) by being thematically selective. As well as considering a different dimension, each of its four chapters focuses its inquiry through a literary source – a memoir, poem, or novel, three of them written within the last hundred years and one composed exactly four hundred years ago, in 1623. Each chapter treats the issues that arise from that particular metaphor of the eucharist as a kind of conversation with the everyday stuff of modern living. I have been wary of coming to conclusions, but have tried to be morally decisive when I have encountered this generation's culturally habituated cruelties, opposing them with Christ's invitation to the disciplines of love.

My mistakes are all my own, but my obligation and gratitude to others – some for detailed advice, others for a passing reference or a piece of writing or music I didn't know – is great. I name them here. Rachel Blanchflower, Nicola Bown, Stephen Brooker, Andrew Brown, Fenella Cannell, Sarah Coakley, Eamon Duffy, the late Jenny Gage, the late Eric Griffiths, Sam Inglis, Alan Jacobs, Victoria Johnson, Helen King, Devin McLachlan, Matthew McNaught, Judith Maltby, Rachel Mann, Bernice Martin, the late David Martin, Magnus Martin, China Mieville, David Newton, Jitesh Patel, Martyn Percy, Angela Rayner, Adam Roberts, Alec Ryrie, Martin Seeley, Adam Seligman, Theodora Spufford: thank you. To the colleagues alongside whom the daily eucharist is offered at Ely Cathedral, Mark Bonney, James Garrard, James Reveley: thank you. To the many members of that cathedral community who trusted me with their thoughts and apprehensions of the eucharist, within and outside the pandemic: thank you. To Christine Smith and Rachel Geddes at the Canterbury Press for your patience and encouragement: thank you.

Finally, constantly and always, to Francis Spufford, without whose loving persistence I might never remember that there is more to my calling than the more-or-less faithful duties of each day. Thank you.

I

The Point of the Eucharist

Modernity and metaphysics

In 2017 the American poet Patricia Lockwood published her memoir, *Priestdaddy*. Towards the end of it, more or less in passing, she holds up to her readers a vision of the eucharist.

Lockwood, described by the *New York Times* as 'the smutty metaphor queen of Lawrence, Kansas',[1] doesn't seem the obvious first voice for contemplation of the sacrament. She came to prominence in 2013 with her witty, painful poem 'Rape Joke', which spoke powerfully – more powerfully than she expected – to a world in which rape is the dark, unacknowledged and mostly unredressed rite of passage for a grimly high percentage of young women.[2] Lockwood's 2017 memoir, an account of her growing up as one of five children to a Lutheran pastor turned Roman Catholic priest, directs a similarly intense, vivid, funny,

---

1 https://nytimes.com/2014/06/01/magazine/the-smutty-metaphor-queen-of-lawrence-kansas.html (accessed 24.2.2023).

2 https://www.theawl.com/2013/07/patricia-lockwood-rape-joke/ (accessed 24.2.2023).

Globally, almost one in three women has experienced rape (this figure does not include sexual harassment). Less than half of these are reported to the police. In the UK in 2020 the number of reported rapes resulting in either prosecution or conviction fell to the lowest in any year for which data exists. According to Sarah Green, the director of End Violence Against Women, 'rape is effectively decriminalised. What else can you call a 1 in 70 chance of a prosecution?' https://www.unwomen.org/en/what-we-do/ending-violence-against-women/facts-and-figures (accessed 24.2.2023); https://www.theguardian.com/society/2020/jul/30/convictions-fall-record-low/england-wales-prosecutions (accessed 24.2.2023).

anguished vision outwards on the world. Lockwood, in prose and in poetry, is never abstract: all her effects are physical, visceral, felt with and in a body of constant and shifting passions. Sex is her go-to theme for thinking about other things. And she does an awful lot of thinking.

Towards the end of her memoir, she and her husband Jason pay a visit to her parents. At the same time, a new monstrance arrives for her father in the post from London. But Jason, a former Baptist, has no idea what a monstrance is. So she tells him:

> a monstrance is a sort of twenty-four-karat solid gold sunburst that holds the body of the Lord. There's a window at the center and a thousand rays reach out of it in every direction, so it stands on the altar like a permanent dawn. The word 'monstrance' means 'to show', and when I read it, up rises that round image of the bread through the glass – bread that my own father had consecrated, at the climax of a metaphor that is more than a metaphor, at the moment when real time intersects with eternity. How to explain this moment to someone who never believed it, could never believe it? That bells ring, that the universe kneels, that what happened enters into the house of what is always happening, and sits with it together, and eats at its table.[3]

At this moment, Patricia Lockwood is doing her own piece of showing. She lifts up to us a *something* she has doubts about being able to realize. 'How to explain this moment to someone who never believed it, could never believe it?' she asks. She's being a translator, a kind of wry, indigenous interpreter for the incomprehensibly strange. She has a foot in both worlds. There is the old world in which bread changes the universe, and there is the new – in which it never could, and never has.

Lockwood's, then, is a powerful voice through which to think about what, in the eucharist, is real. Fluent in more than

---

3 Patricia Lockwood, *Priestdaddy: A Memoir* (London: Allen Lane, 2017), pp. 330–1.

one language, with a split sensibility, Lockwood's imagination skitters with sceptical, internet-shaped irony. As a poet, her business is holding words up to the world our bodies know: she does this in funny and inconvenient and silly and tragic and occasionally joyful ways. Yet, shaped by and steeped in an old faith, she is also an involuntary witness to the unseen universe of ontological change.

Patricia Lockwood's history and character make her handily spectacular as an exemplar of the culturally divided self. Yet that is just what she is – an exemplar, not an exception. She makes especially visible the fissure shared by all modern selfhoods, the deep gap between incompatible ways of defining what is 'real'. We moderns have particular trouble with intangibles – by which I mean beliefs whose basis is imaginary or invisible rather than empirical. (Please have a little patience with that word 'imaginary', a word we tend to use as a synonym for 'not real', and consider whether 'not real' is really a very satisfactory or complete description for the reach of human perception.) We have all, believers and non-believers alike, grown up understanding that our deepest trust must be in scepticism. We should test every thought. What we should test every thought *against* isn't quite so self-evident.

Living with Hamlet's Ghost

'There is nothing either good or bad but thinking makes it so', remarked Prince Hamlet – though, as with much that he says, it's not clear whether either he, or we, should believe him.[4] In the plot of Shakespeare's *Hamlet*, the apparently empirical evidence of sight and hearing sits on a tricky border between the internal workings of the mind and the outward activity of the world, a border so ambiguous that the audience quickly learns to trust nothing. The Ghost may or may not be 'real'.

---

4 William Shakespeare, *Hamlet* (1600), 2.2.239–40, New Cambridge Shakespeare, ed. Philip Edwards (1985).

And the Ghost may or may not be truthful. The separateness of the Ghost's reality from the unreliable workings of Hamlet's perceptions is never certain. In this ambiguity, Prince Hamlet's outlook is indeed 'early modern'.

It is one we 'late moderns' might recognize. For, in spite of the fierce grip with which we clutch our rationality, the unstable relationship between mind and world that permeates *Hamlet* hands down to us a haunting that we also must endure. This too is a Ghost of what may or may not be real, a Ghost who whispers to us that our perceptions may be liars. This Ghost shows itself in our relationship to the past, especially to memory and to the dead. It shows itself in the authority we assign to the inner self as the ultimate judge of what is real, 'authentic' or sincere (as in the massively conflicted area of gender identity); *and* it also shows itself in the many challenges to that inner authority.[5] It shows itself in our huge cultural fascination with imagined worlds in which words have the power to change the shape of physical objects and states, flourishing within the genres of fantasy, gaming, anime, cosplay and even SF. Such worlds are safely defined as fictive, but are also immersive, powerful. In certain areas – for example in online sex or indeed online worship – the apparently clear boundaries between the physical world and its artificial representation are ambiguous, blurred. Images and persons are not completely distinct, either in law or in feeling.

Hamlet's Ghost shows itself in the suspicion with which we approach anything that claims a universal 'supernatural' truth, but also in the eagerness with which we embrace the bittier, more controllable promises of 'spirituality'. It shows itself in

---

5 To quote the anthropologist Webb Keane: 'The dematerialization of religion and the dematerialization of the person understood in more secular terms go hand in hand. According to [Charles] Taylor, the main current of literary and philosophical visions of the modern self centers on modes of self-consciousness that depend on the assumption that consciousness can be fully disembodied and the self not placed in the world along with other natural things.' Webb Keane, *Christian Moderns* (University of California Press, 2007), ch.2 n.19.

the conflict and uncertainty we show in how to define what is 'real' in a world dominated by internet representation and assertion. It shows itself in a persistent, fascinated and terrified cultural fantasy in which empirical realities reveal themselves to be deliberate, cruel fictions hiding a grimmer truth (whether by this we mean *The Matrix*, *The Truman Show*, *Black Mirror*, or their many, many precursors and spinoffs).

The Ghost shows itself in our anguished relationship with 'mental health' and in our troubled relationship with our actual bodies. It shows itself in the difficult negotiations within medicine on the borders between physical and mental disease, and within the legal system on the borders between transgressive and emotionally wounded behaviour. It shows itself in our fascination with the limits of the empirical, the points where our physical senses prove to be unreliable witnesses. It shows itself in our continuing doubt as to whether such terms as 'good' or 'bad' can even retain a stable collective meaning at all; *and* it shows itself in our inability to manage without them.

That's quite a list.

Invisible goods

Everyone, religious or not, has a few items sitting in the 'intangible reality' category, whether that's love, or decency, or the common good, or self-belief, or some other social imaginary. Often we call them 'values' (though we seldom dare to ask what exactly they measure). It is simply not possible *only* to admit the reality of testable phenomena; nobody can really manage to live that way, though a few have tried. The influence of logical positivism permeates modern culture but it does so very inconsistently. On the whole, we modern human beings continue to believe in a motley, self-selected rag-bag of unprovable stuff, because we can't help it. Cut off from each other during the pandemic, or shaken by the vast slippery range of what-to-trust, huge numbers of us believed sheer nonsense even as we proffered the 'science' that declared our beliefs to be tested by a laudable scepticism: these are the 'rabbit holes' of conspiracy theory that make a terrifying world intelligible, controllable, communal. Yet we also find our own tendency to belief unjustifiable.

To believe and not-believe at the same time is a profoundly fracturing experience. Yet every modern person – including the kind with religious belief – is always doing it.

You could put our problem this way.

1 We hold that our information about what is real is derived from physical evidence, direct or extrapolated, from the world we encounter through our senses. Bread is always and only bread.

2 But we also hold that the shaping power of thoughts, feelings and ideas is authoritative enough to govern, reorder and, if necessary, override the dumb, obdurate evidence of our physicality. Bread is **not** always and only bread.

Each of these positions notices something true about how embodied, self-conscious human beings make sense of the world. But they don't fit together. 'Metaphysical' is just *not talking* to 'physical' – to use some old-fashioned categories. We cannot see ourselves whole.

Faith and the body

I've said this is a problem for everyone, the irreligious as much as the religious. And it is. But, for now, I'm going to concentrate on the problems it poses for the modern but believing Christian – or for any modern person seriously considering Christian belief. For the Christian, the distrust of physics for metaphysics is a massive issue, because Christianity makes claims that join the two together intimately. Christianity is *incarnational*, deliberately empirical in its claims, binding the invisible to the visible in the historical, material humanity of Jesus in space and time. Its spiritual claims, therefore, are inseparable from the physical world of bodies and behaviours and actions.

It's true that Jesus himself, drawing upon one strand of his Judaic tradition, stressed that the convictions of the heart, its disposition towards God and neighbour, carried more authority than physical practices or behaviours. But Jesus also, and most unsettlingly, tightened the bond between soul and body. His healing miracles seem to collapse the distinction between physical and spiritual restoration. This close alignment of bodily with spiritual healing finds powerful imitative expression in many burgeoning versions of modern Christianity – mostly Pentecostal/charismatic ones in the global majority world – but it is hugely problematic for post-Enlightenment cultures such as ours.[6] During the pandemic times, it has been especially and painfully jarring to try to set spiritual and bodily needs in align-

---

6 Work on the twentieth-century charismatic revival – including healing by faith – within Anglicanism reveals this unease very swiftly, for example in the life and work of David Watson and Michael Harper, and the history of the Fountain Trust. In the next, post-denominational generation, Matthew McNaught's prizewinning book *Immanuel* (London: Fitzcarraldo Editions, 2022) explores the ultimately destructive relationship between the restorationist church in which he grew up in Winchester in the 1990s and the healing/exorcism ministry of the Pentecostal Nigerian 'Synagogue Church of All Nations' (SCOAN). In *Immanuel* McNaught details, passionately and precisely, the fierce tension between the post-Enlightenment 'rational' world of late capitalist modernity and the roilingly interconnected world of body and spirit in one of its global majority Pentecostal versions. Almost as an aside, he brings a similar partly-distanced clarity to bear on the individualistic belief-structures of modern psychological healing practices, of which he is a practitioner: 'The problem was not just the alphabet soup of overlapping disorders, or the fact that some people seemed to be possessed by half a dozen of these entities at once. It was the assumption that healthy normality was our default setting, and excesses of suffering were simply deviations to be corrected ... that our human predicament was something other than tragic, something other than catastrophic ... I'd grown weary of the individualist view of the self that lay behind our training: the psyche as something separate, to be improved and calibrated by its owner. It seemed that people's suffering was often more a result of disconnect – from purpose, from others, from aspects of themselves – than the symptoms of a neatly delineated disorder. There were few forces as tyrannical as an atomized mind turned against itself' (pp. 49–50).

ment, when the medical requirements of social distancing and physical isolation stripped away so much of the soul's comfort.

Yet the Christian hope does align soul and body. Jesus's redemptive work was a bodily event, but the restoration it promised was also spiritual. He offered himself, physically broken by the political machine, as a sacrifice, in order to liberate the human soul into reconciliation with the Creator of all. But sacrifices don't work rationally. They work symbolically. It is not actually self-evident how one man's death re-aligns the whole of humanity, which is why straplines that say 'he died for you' don't have automatic impact on populations trained only in utilitarian and consequentialist thinking.

And the resurrection is a differently messy phenomenon. It isn't some kind of metaphor. It's not even, to use Patricia Lockwood's words, a 'metaphor that is more than a metaphor'. It's *bodily*: a body, once dead, now living, proclaiming himself, there and then, as the sign for the intimate re-joining of mortal humanity with the eternal, intangible being of God.

Resurrection re-knits, renews, *re-members*, the life of memory with life in the world of time and space. The risen Jesus ate, drank, cooked and served breakfast, walked a day's journey, broke bread, touched and was touched.[7] There is no hint in the Gospels that his resurrection was 'just' an *idea*.

But, after only a few weeks of this, Jesus *did* vanish physically from the world. We mark that at the end of the Easter Season, in the Feast of the Ascension – though only one of the Gospel writers, Luke (writing both in the Gospel of Luke and in the Acts of the Apostles), securely places Jesus's ascension at the end of his forty days of physical resurrection.[8] Instead of his tangible body Jesus promised (in words spoken in the Gospel of John) a companion – as powerful and untouchable as wind or flame – called the 'Holy Spirit', and he left behind him a trail of human-told stories and human-made rituals that made, and

---

7 Matthew 28.8–10, 16–20; Mark 16.9–15; Luke 24.13–end; John 20.13–29; John 21.

8 Luke 24.50–end; Acts 1.1–11.

make, claims to contain him and yet also to be inadequate to contain him.[9]

For all Christians beyond that first generation, Jesus, risen and ascended and awaited, is always both here and not-here, remembered and expected and yet abiding, yesterday and today and for ever.[10] When we celebrate the eucharist, Jesus, the host at the feast where we are guests, is in physical terms both absent *and* present. '*What happened* enters into the house of *what is always happening*, and sits with it together, and eats at its table.'

'An emptiness that asks to be filled'

All rituals of worship, Christian or not, are events on a border-line between physicality and the unseen world. All rituals of worship treat this borderline as porous, and the rituals are modes for crossing it, for bringing the one into the other. The eucharist does this work too, but its border crossing is a charged, unstable experience. Its meanings are impossible for the human-made ritual to control, especially as Christians themselves are deeply split about what those meanings are and how they happen. One provocative way of putting this is to say that it's not totally clear – from the inside as well as the outside – whether the eucharistic community, when it meets together to encounter the presence of God, is doing a world-changing *something*, or a private, reflective, rather undramatic *nothing*.

Now I'll say it another way. When we put together Jesus's physical absence with our inherited modern ambivalence about the power of symbolic action, we exert a huge pressure on the rite of the eucharist. How *can* we come close to Jesus, human and divine, now taken from the world and awaited eschatolog-ically? Is the sacramental bread our means to see, touch and taste God, or just a way of invoking a completely inward – and perhaps slippery and deniable – reality of thought and feeling?

---

9 John 16.7–14; John 21.24–end.
10 Hebrews 13.8.

A good many Christians *also* believe that bread is only bread, even though they may at the same time believe that they might be transformed by a powerful inner event. Yet they know that the choked avenues of emotion don't offer reliable messages, and that they will probably be left asking, '*Did* anything happen just now? How will I know?'

It's not clear, in a rite that celebrates a physical body in its absence, what irreducible basics the rite requires. Do we *need* to gather physically, when our absent Lord is present everywhere? Do we need to specify a place, a time, a physical community, when he brings with him the unlocated benefits of eternity? How quickly will we, like King Lear's older daughters, strip our ceremony of symbolic power until we move from providing the minimal signs of honour to providing no signs of honour at all, because they are 'not needed'? Why have a ritual at all? 'What need one'?[11] As with online sex, how far does the communion ritual *need* an irreducible Other to be efficacious, or would it work perfectly well without? Does joy lie with that utterly real Person, or is it all confined within *the way it makes me feel*? Is it all about us, really, with nothing beyond but the knowledge of a vast illusion? At the point of communion, is the soul met – or hopelessly alone? Blue pill, anyone?

At what point will we find that calling all absence presence turns God's presence into absence? Or is it that we are living in a world in which the Christians who went before us have already done that, and now the churches are empty? The anthropologist Webb Keane, in his influential book *Christian Moderns*, describes the anxiety of his Dutch Calvinist missionaries as they slowly convert the inhabitants of the Indonesian island of Sumba. They've successfully persuaded their converts that their sacred places are not sacred, that their sacred rituals are meaningless, that all that is needed to be close to God is an inward faith. But the missionaries are left with a nagging worry. Did they empty out the physical world so much, leaving

---

11 William Shakespeare, *King Lear* (1607), 2.4.261, Arden Shakespeare, ed. Kenneth Muir (1972).

only the slender thread of inner conviction, in order to pave the way for the Sumba to discover unbelief, to redraw their structures of cultural meaning in terms of the economic, capitalist estimates of material value that arrived along with Protestant Christianity? Have they shut the way between the sacred and the material world? Conversion, writes one of Sumba's later missionaries, unhappily, 'creates here an emptiness that asks to be filled'.[12]

'O, reason not the need.'[13] It isn't *God's* needs that are met in ritual. Jesus didn't ask us to 'do this in remembrance of me' because *he* needed it. He asks this of us because the need is ours: body and soul, we long to be not lost.

I am not setting up to solve these dilemmas. I'm as compromised and conflicted as anyone else born into our time and place. I can't see clearly around or outside the shifty, opaque and inconsistent ways of knowing that shaped us all. Yet the thing – 'that holy thing'[14] as the herald of the incarnation, Gabriel, put it – that I have put my trust into declaring that I know, the thing that brings tangible and intangible truth together into one, is held up to humanity and then broken, shared and consumed in the sacrament of the altar – in the eucharist.

How *can* the eucharist hold the heart of meaning? *Can* rituals invoke God? Why would God come? Across my lifetime I have read accounts of the eucharist which confidently claim transformative divine meaning for it, and across my lifetime the eucharist has been the default setting for regular Christian worship. I have been to drab eucharists, clunky eucharists,

---

12 Louis Onvlee, 'De Betekenis van Vee en Veebezit' in *Cultuur als antwoord*, 1973, pp. 10–26 quoted in translation in Webb Keane, *Christian Moderns* (2007), p. 247.

13 Shakespeare, *King Lear* (1607), 2.4.262, Arden Shakespeare, ed. Kenneth Muir. King Lear is pointing out to his loveless daughter Regan that bare need is not the only reason for offering a Father the signs of care, honour and attention.

14 Luke 1.35 in the King James translation of 1611, where the angel says to Mary 'that holy thing that shall be born of thee shall be called the Son of God'.

frankly embarrassing eucharists; I have been to hieratic eucharists, intimate eucharists, village eucharists, mourning eucharists;
I have been to eucharists that were feasts of the senses and to
eucharists of indigestible dryness. I have been bored, infuriated,
restless, indifferent, anguished, opened up, closed down, un-
settled, even occasionally joyful. I've wept on receiving the
Host and I've felt nothing at all. In this, my experience mirrors
that of most Christians for whom the sacraments are significant. And, in this, I am in a minority within this nation that is
not only astonishingly small, but is getting smaller all the time.
The eucharistic community is shrinking in my culture and looks
as if it might die. Sacramental Christian worship is *on the wane*.

So I can't speak in the language and idiom of Gregory Dix,
or Kenneth Stevenson, or Austin Farrer, or Michael Ramsey, or
John MacQuarrie or Michael Welker or even Karen O'Donnell.
Their confidence that the culture that shapes us will recognize
the eucharist's significance is one I cannot share. I've got to
listen to Patricia Lockwood, who knows, with part of herself,
that it's a pointless and alien ritual that sounds like cannibalism
and feels like watching paint dry. Yet at the same time another
part of her continues to ask, *is this eternity breaking in? What
has the invisible world to impart to time, space, bodies?*

The point of the eucharist

In the course of this book, I will be asking questions of the
ritual of eucharist. Some of those questions are, if you like, 'historical' ones – because there is actually an intimate relationship
between our split modern sensibility about what is 'real' and
the bitter, bloody historical debates about how and what the
eucharist could mean.[15] Some of those questions are literary,

---

15 This is a subject of its own, but here are some landmarks: R. H.
Tawney, *Religion and the Rise of Capitalism* (John Murray, 1926); J. P.
Singh Uberoi, *Science and Culture* (Oxford University Press, 1978); Eamon
Duffy, *The Stripping of the Altars: Traditional Religion in England 1400–
1580* (Yale University Press, 1992); Webb Keane, *Christian Moderns:*

others anthropological. Still others try to look attentively at individual experience of eucharist and how it is mediated. The whole enterprise is, to use a fancy word, epistemological. I am framing a question about what we know of the reality of eucharist in the light of the dissociated nature of our usual knowledge systems. I can't promise to get as far as an answer.

I've chosen a geometrical metaphor as a way of navigating this, which is why this book is called *The Eucharist in Four Dimensions*. This seems fitting for a rite that joins the physical world to the invisible truths of heaven by means of a remembered, broken body. This opening section is asking about the eucharist's 'point' – that is, it locates eucharist on a map of meaning. Later on, I look at two-dimensional textual and screen-based manifestations of the rite, and at the anxious dominance of linear argument over its gifts. Further on still, space and bodies (the third dimension), and then time and memory (the fourth), come into prominence.

Of course, these geometrical divisions are artificial. You can't talk about the point of eucharist and leave out everything it's made of in terms of words and time and space and bodies and memory. You can't discuss online eucharists or textual organization without thinking about the physical actions of persons in a place. And you can't talk about the way the eucharist enacts meaning as theatre does without looking backwards and forwards along a *temporal* line. Theatre, after all, is made of events happening in time. The metaphor of the four dimensions

---

Freedom and Fetish in the Mission Encounter (University of California Press, 2007); Charles Taylor, *A Secular Age* (Harvard University Press, 2007); Brad S. Gregory, *The Unintended Reformation: How a Religious Revolution Secularised Society* (Harvard University Press, 2012); Alec Ryrie, *Being Protestant in Reformation Britain* (Oxford University Press, 2013) and *Unbelievers: An Emotional History of Doubt* (HarperCollins, 2019); David Martin, *Ruin and Restoration: on Violence, Liturgy and Reconciliation* (Routledge, 2016); and from a more explicitly literary angle, Sophie Read, *Real Presence: Eucharist and the Poetic Imagination in Early Modern England* (Cambridge University Press, 2013). In early modern studies, Catholic historians are more absolute for a straight causal link between reformation and secularization than Protestant ones.

is only a way of examining the layers of something whose layers are never separated. But to look at them one by one will let us see the eucharist's elements, and the connections between them.

So what *is* the 'point' of the eucharist?

In geometrical terms, a point is a locator within a space, though paradoxically it takes up no space itself. Strictly speaking it is not even one-dimensional until its location is joined to another, different, location to make a line.

In the figurative sense of ordinary speech, a 'point' is one of the many spatial metaphors we use to order our thoughts. The 'point' of a discourse is signalled to be the heart of its meaning, a figurative place to locate the source of, or the conclusion to, an idea. If you say to someone else, 'No, you're missing *the point*', you mean that they've left out, ignored or looked away from the heart of the meaning as you see it.

Counterpoint and fracture

However, 'points' tend to arise as part of a dispute as to what might be that defining heart of meaning. So as well as the person making the point, another will be making a 'counter-point' that aims to re-define what is most important. The relation between point and counterpoint may be a dance or a battle, a joined or a broken line. (As well as its significance for formal, verbal argument, there is of course a whole branch of musical structure based on this premise.)

Can we learn anything about the 'point' of the eucharist through this metaphor? I think we can. It comes, though, with difficulties, because the dance between points that makes up the theological disputes on the eucharist is deeply and irreconcilably fractured, part of a history of bitter, internecine, ideological conflict. Its lines are broken, and with it, potentially, the lines of communication between participants in the act of worship.

What are the differing points of this broken line?

For some, the point of the eucharist will be unity. Full participation in the ritual knits together the Body of Christ, a body corporate of people joined in community. As the body of worshippers comes to the threshold of the central eucharistic event, it affirms its unitary identity in the section called 'the Peace' (sometimes attended with kisses, handclasping, even hugs). Many of the scripturally-derived exhortations in Anglican liturgy that herald the exchange of the Peace underline a unity hovering somewhere between an identity divinely gifted and something more difficult to realize – collective harmony as a worked-for, costly (and probably fleeting) achievement. 'As members of one Body you are called to peace', says one exhortation[16]. Yet 'We are all one in Christ Jesus', affirms another.[17] Perhaps the most commonly used of all contains both perceptions – the invisible truth that the people of God are 'one body'; but also the collective work towards 'peace' that begins to knit together the visibly and continually scattered collection of people that makes up that Body:

> We are the body of Christ. In the one Spirit we were all baptized into one body. Let us then pursue all that makes for peace and builds up our common life.[18]

For others – regardless of their formal views on religious unity – eucharist divides. It divides the holy from the unregenerate or the unready. These are not necessarily judgements between believers and unbelievers. Many who confess and call themselves Christians will not be invited to eat at some iterations of the holy table, either because of differing theologies of communion, or because of institutional judgements about an individual's mode of life, or because the person is deemed not yet to understand enough to receive the benefits of eucharistic participation. Here is an historical example from the instructions in the 1549 *Book of Common Prayer*:

---

16 Cf Colossians 3.15.
17 Cf Galatians 3.28.
18 Cf 1 Corinthians 12.13, Ephesians 4.3.

> So if any of those [coming to communion] be an open and no-
> torious evil liver, so that the congregacion by him is offended,
> or have done any wrong to his neighbours by worde or dede,
> the Curate shall call him, and advertise him, not in any wise to
> presume to the lordes table, until he have amended his former
> naughtie life.[19]

But a 'naughtie life' is not a necessary precondition for exclu-
sion from the holy table. The Roman Catholic Church accepts
no other Christian denomination into communion with it. Were
I to go to worship God at Patricia Lockwood's father's church,
I would watch the bells ring and the universe kneel from behind
a locked fence marked 'NO ENTRY'.[20]

Liturgically, within the rite of eucharist itself, both division
and unity are central elements. For distribution, there must be
fraction: to be shared, the blessed bread must be broken; for
the community to be unified, it must also be demarcated. At the
Fraction, the breaking of the bread immediately before communion, the priest in the Anglican rite may declare: 'We break
this bread to share in the body of Christ.' The worshippers
reply: 'Though we are many, we are one body, because we all
share in one bread.'[21] Their unity is realized in the shattering of
the Host into pieces.

Then, another broken line.

For some, the point of the eucharist will be the transformation brought about, by the power of the Holy Spirit, upon

---

19 *The Book of Common Prayer: The Texts of 1549, 1559, and 1662*,
ed. Brian Cummings (Oxford: Oxford University Press, 2013), p. 19.

20 And, of course, that extends to a division about who would count
as an efficacious president for a communion service. In the 1924 novel
The Counterplot by the Roman Catholic author Hope Mirrlees, which
has its own reasons for being interested in the sacrament, her main character Teresa, also Roman Catholic, remarks 'Bad writers are like priests
who haven't proper Orders – they can scream *hoc est corpus* till they are
hoarse, but nothing happens' (p. x).

21 See https://www.churchofengland.org/prayer-and-worship/worship-
texts-and-resources/common-worship/holy-communion-service#mm
7c2 (accessed 13.2.2023).

the material elements of bread and wine: the 'real presence' of Christ in the elements. Such worshippers will treat those elements with special reverence, and the physicality of the acts of eating and drinking will therefore matter a great deal. Every consecrated crumb or drop contains God; every consecrated crumb or drop must therefore be ritually consumed or its continuing presence in the violent and indifferent world will exert dishonour upon it.

For others, the point of eucharist will be an internal recollection, a memorial of an act once done long ago and now over, which Jesus enjoined his followers to remember. For those people the elements of bread and wine are nothing much in themselves, and the eating and drinking, important as it is, is less the point than the internal transformation it engenders through the vehicle of Jesus's command: 'Do this in remembrance of me'. The most significant representative of this memorialist position, the sixteenth-century reformer Huldrich Zwingli, separates the physicality of the bread from the power of Jesus's command like this: 'In [Jesus's] ... words, "This is my body", the word "this" means the bread, and the word "body" means the body which was put to death for us. Therefore the word "is" cannot be taken literally, for the bread is not the body.'[22] As Zwingli frames it, the obedience of the people in consuming the bread and drinking the wine makes no difference to the bread and wine itself, whatever transformative effect it may have on the souls of those remembering Jesus.

His reforming contemporary Martin Luther, whose view is not memorialist and who, like his forebears, perceives the bread and wine as subject to a true change, has this in common with Zwingli: he still locates the transformative power of that eucharistic moment not in the elements but to Jesus's words as recorded in scripture, assigning to them a trans-temporal power:

---

22 Huldrich Zwingli, *On the Lord's Supper* (1531), LCC 24:225.

You won't chew or slurp him [God] like the cabbage or soup on your table unless he will it. He has now become incomprehensible; you can't touch him even if he is in your bread – unless, that is, he binds himself to you and summons you to a special table with his word and with his word points out to you the bread you should eat. This he does in the Last Supper.[23]

In modern Anglicanism (and indeed in its liturgies from the 1540s onwards) a good deal of effort has been put into blurring the difference across the range of views between real presence and memorial iteration, and today's faithful are implicitly, yet forcefully, invited to look away from them, because the history of that particular difference is a bloody one.

And yet another fracture of perception. For some the act of eucharist contains within it the suffering of Calvary. The holy meal prefigures the breaking of God's body upon the cross. Seventeenth-century manuals of eucharistic devotion would ponder the violence involved in the material production of bread and wine – the pulverized grain, the trodden grape, the action of tongue and teeth upon the elements. One such manual was *The Whole Duty of a Communicant*, and it was explicit about the link between the everyday violence of bodily need and the unique violence of God's death:

The *Bread* after it passeth much violence of the Mill, hand, and fire, is made wholesome for Food, and the *Wine* after it hath endured the torture of the Press is prepared for drink; *the body and blood of Christ*, not whole, entire and unsufferable, but Crucified and Broken in his Passion, when he did undergo the burthen of the *sins of the world*, and was under the pressure of the Justice of God, and Sacrificed *for the*

---

23 Martin Luther, 'Vom Abendmahl Christi, Bekenntnis' (1528), quoted in Phyllis Mack, *Visionary Women: Ecstatic Prophecy in Seventeenth Century England* (University of California Press, 1994), p. 21.

redemption of mankind, under this consideration is received by the believing.[24]

The many readers of that seventeenth-century manual found it ordinary to walk a straight line, imaginatively, from the every-day, necessary force intrinsic to processing and consuming food to the saving gift of Christ's crucifixion, the lethal pressure upon his physical frame, the effusion of blood and water from his wounded side.

For others the eating metaphor works quite differently. The feast is a heavenly one, a foretaste of a banquet in which nothing and no-one will ever suffer any more, and every tear is dried. Rather than contemplating time and gravity breaking eternity in the dying body of Jesus, the eschatological worship-per instead contemplates eternity as it mends the ravages of time and gravity. The earliest worshippers of the first Christian centuries tended to this eschatological view, living as they did in a world where Christian meanings attracted persecution and where, therefore, public humiliation and judicial killings were redefined as doors to eternal joy. From the fourth century onwards, when Constantine had embedded Christian meaning into the wider culture, rather than having to re-enact the drama of the Passion in their own experience, later liturgies looked to and adored a historicized, temporal and spatial Jesus from an imagined distance through the figure of the cross. For them, the repetition of Jesus's death was inscribed in the circular sym-bolic actions of the church year, from which the private events of their lives could be safely distinct. In Gregory Dix's words,

As the church became at home in the world, she became rec-onciled to *time.* The eschatological emphasis in the eucharist inevitably faded. It ceased to be regarded primarily as a rite

24 [John Gauden], *The Whole Duty of a Communicant* (London, 1685), p. 13. This bestselling text ran to 14 editions between its first publication in 1681 and its last edition in 1723. See Ian Green, *Print and Protestantism in Early Modern England* (Oxford University Press, 2000), p. 621.

which manifested and secured the *eternal consequences* of redemption ... momentarily [transporting] ... those who took part in it beyond the alien and hostile world of time into the Kingdom of God ... Instead, the eucharist came to be thought of primarily as the representation, the re-enactment before God, of the *historical process* of redemption, of the historical events of the crucifixion and resurrection of Jesus by which redemption had been achieved. And the pliable idea of *anamnesis* ['not-forgetting'] was there to ease the transition.[25]

The 'point' of the eucharist, then, is embattled, a dance of contrasting points. This rite of communion contains the irreconcilable.

The fractured soul

'I come not to bring peace, but a sword', said Jesus in one of his wryer, grimmer moments, and in this prophecy he was entirely correct.[26] The history of eucharistic theory, taking it just since the Reformation, is a history of fraction. Not just of violent ideological divisions, though it is certainly that, but of the fracturing of the modern sensibility itself. The point has been made by a good many people in a good many different intellectual disciplines, but here it is articulated in 1978, in the words of J. P. Singh Uberoi, sociologist and philosophical anthropologist, in his influential book *Science and Culture*, a critique of hegemonic Western systems of thought. This is how he analyses Zwingli's assertion that the verb 'to be' must be understood figuratively in Jesus's words 'This is my body':

Zwingli insisted that in the utterance 'This is my body' *(Hoc est corpus meum)* the existential word 'is' *(est)* was to be

---

25 The point is made by Gregory Dix in his chapter, 'The Sanctification of Time', in *The Shape of the Liturgy* (Dacre Press, 1945), p. 305.
26 Matthew 10.34.

understood, not in a real, literal and corporeal sense, but only in a symbolical, historical or social sense ... by stating the issue and forcing it in terms of dualism, or more properly double monism, Zwingli had discovered or invented the modern concept of time in which every event was either spiritual and mental or corporeal and material but no event was or could be both at once ... spirit, word and sign had finally parted company for man at Marburg in 1529.[27]

Uberoi went on to argue that the Zwinglian categories became the basis for modern Western scientific thought, a system in which there was no necessary connection between symbol and reality; one, therefore, in which all ritual became potentially empty of meaning.

Sound familiar? Is that a world you recognize? It may not *be* true but it is frequently assumed to be true that ritual does nothing and that words are not acts. These are shaping cultural assumptions for us. And within this world of ours, therefore, there is a question that will occur to most people sooner rather than later. That question is: why worship *at all*? In a knowledge system where the symbolic is divorced from efficacy; where God doesn't need worship either to do or to be; and where nothing and no one is changed by doing it – what's the point?

What is the *point* of the eucharist? Why spend time and energy on this ritual, its meanings as broken by violence as the body it remembers, its hopes of unity as impossible as the resurrection to which it lifts its eyes? Why bother?

I said earlier that the eucharist 'contains the irreconcilable'. You can hear that two ways. It might just mean that the eucharist is made up of contradictions. Or you could subtly shift that meaning's centre of gravity and say instead that eucharist holds those contradictions in bounded relationship through its ritual shaping. The historian of religion Jonathan Zittell Smith argues

---

27 J. P. Singh Uberoi, *Science and Culture* (1978), quoted and discussed in Jonathan Z. Smith, *To Take Place: Towards Theory in Ritual* (University of Chicago Press, 1987), pp. 99–100.

that ritual 'gains force when incongruency is perceived and thought about'.[28] What happens, then, when the brokenness of eucharist – the broken body embedded within it, but also the fissures of its violent history – is enclosed by the actions of its ritual?

'What is' and 'What might be'

For ritual is not only a bridge between physicality and the unseen world. It also sits on the border between the dead weight of *what is* and the quick energy of *what might be*. Both what is and what might be have to find full expression within the ritual enactments of the eucharist. Heartbreak and hope are both its honoured guests, for without the one the other cannot be complete. The participant in eucharist is both a realist and an idealist, able to look steadily at the worst humanity can do and yet still to affirm the primacy of love. Sacred force lies in incongruence.

The ritual mode has been called – by the Jewish scholar Adam Seligman – a 'subjunctive' mode: that is, a mode of possibility that lifts our eyes to a transformation whose way is only, but powerfully, hope. This is not fantasy, but invocation, a bridge between seen and unseen, giving us the life that inscribes meaning upon our bodies, both singly and collectively. Living in the subjunctive mode makes us more than the bald components of our selves. It can happen in small ways – when we thank someone for passing the salt, we posit a world where gratitude is the basis for all transaction, even though we know that this is not the world in which we currently live.

Seligman is careful to stress that ritual, in this mode, is not, or not merely, the enaction of 'harmony' in order to bring harmony about in reality. Rather, his view is that ritual is tragic, its iterations necessary because its vision of harmony will not sur-

---

28 Jonathan Z. Smith, *To Take Place* (University of Chicago Press, 1987), pp. 109–10.

vive the violence of the present. 'If ritual participants thought the world was inherently harmonious, why bother with the rituals? ... From the point of view of ritual, the world is fragmented and fractured. This is why the endless work of ritual is necessary even if that work is always, ultimately, doomed.'[29]

Part of the instability of the Christian vision is that its eschatological underpinning repudiates the repetitions of ritual in favour of a completed act that makes ritual redundant: when Christ's has already been a 'full, perfect and sufficient sacrifice, oblation and satisfaction for the sins of the whole world', what need is there for any iterative act of sacrifice among Christ's people? As the letter to the Hebrews puts it, 'Unlike the other high priests, [Christ] has no need to offer sacrifices day after day, first for his own sins, and then for those of the people; this he did once for all when he offered himself.'[30] And yet here we are, offering sacrifices day after day after day 'in remembrance' – and yet also, in some sense we wince at defining, in reality. And the world in which we offer those sacrifices remains still violent, still fragmented, still fractured, still full of 'darkness and cruel habitations'.[31] Why continue?

This is the promise of the eucharist: that all the physical stuff of life might be changed utterly were bread to become God so that God might nourish us into life by his death. In eucharist, that vision is realized, declared – within the bounds of the ritual – to be present and active, as it cannot be in the mess and violence of the world. Yet the mess and violence of the world, what that mess and violence did to God, is what makes up the ritual of eucharist, so that real and ideal meet within it and kiss each other.

Sacred vision is full of these subjunctives. 'The Lord be with you' operates in a kind of subjunctive mode, wishing an action of blessing that only God can make in the trustful hope that

---

29 Adam B. Seligman and Robert P. Weller, *Ritual and its Consequences: an Essay on the Limits of Sincerity* (Oxford University Press, 2008), p. 31.

30 Hebrews 7.27.

31 Psalm 74.20 (Coverdale).

God will act upon it. Blessings themselves invoke God, but cannot command him. The subjunctive mode is also the mode of prayer and of supplication. Without it – stuck in the prison of 'is' and 'was' without the promise of liberation in what 'might be' – we are poor indeed.

So *this* is the point of the eucharist. In its ritual enactment, we bring into view a world beyond the finite outcomes of the one we know, an eternal world that emerges on the other side of the certainty of death. In it, a story of loss is re-membered as restoration, a story of dying becomes a kind of rebirth. In it, violence becomes nourishment, and a tragic sorrow inexhaustible joy. A world where we celebrate the eucharist is one in which bread indeed changes the universe, because the maker of the universe declares that it may.

Would you not long to be part of such a world?

2

Flat Eucharist:
Schemes and Screens

Adoration

In 1920, the Russian poet Osip Mandelstam wrote a poem on the adoration of the eucharist. Of Jewish heritage, and drawn to Christianity, Mandelstam was persecuted, partially silenced and eventually destroyed under Stalin.

> There: the Eucharist, a gold sun
> hung in the air – an instant of splendour.
> Here nothing should be heard but the Greek syllables –
> the whole world held in the hands like a plain apple.
>
> The solemn height of the holy office; the light
> of July in the rotunda under the cupola;
> so that we may sigh from full hearts, outside time,
> for that little meadow where time does not flow.
>
> And the Eucharist spreads like an eternal noon;
> all partake of it, everyone plays and sings,
> and in each one's eyes the sacred vessel
> brims over with inexhaustible joy.[1]

Mandelstam's eucharist is a eucharist of the eye. It begins with an image that is also the world's light source: a 'gold sun'. The

---

1 Untitled poem from *Tristia* (1922), in *Osip Mandelstam: Selected Poems*, trans. Clarence Brown and W. S. Merwin (Athenaeum, 1973; Penguin, 1977), p. 55.

word translated here as 'eucharist' is *daronositsa*, meaning 'gift holder'; the name is given to the Host itself (the bread holding the gift) as well as to the thing that contains and shows the Host. Sometimes the *daronositsa* looks like a little cupboard, but it can also take a form closely resembling the Roman Catholic monstrance, with (as Patricia Lockwood puts it) its 'window at the center and a thousand rays reach[ing] out of it in every direction, so it stands on the altar like a permanent dawn'. *Daronositsa*, then, is both the thing itself and the container for the thing, as the gold sun is both a thing in itself and a source for the light that enables life.

By the end of the poem's first verse, the golden disc of light has become what light falls upon: the round world, concentrated into the edible, everyday sphere of a 'plain apple' held between the hands. There is a beautiful, spare economy to that image; it folds up all the strength and sweetness of created things into the archetypal fruit, held in hands that are both divine and human.

Still, though, it retains the qualities of a sun. It feeds through light, spreading its rays out 'like an eternal noon' to enter the 'all' who 'partake'. Its shape and substance illuminate those who watch it through the physicality of their own seeing: 'in thy light we see light', as the psalmist sings.[2] The roundness of sun and of world become, at the poem's close, the fleshly orb of the eye, brimming with tears like a chalice overflowing.

Mandelstam's poem contains and displays the eucharist as the *daronositsa* contains and displays the bread that contains and displays Christ. It is epiphanic, a showing. Its first move is to direct the eye to see the holy thing; its last to make the eye itself into a fountain of grace. Somewhere behind that final image there may be those gazers in the prophecy of Zechariah who 'open a fountain' for the house of David, weeping 'as for an only child', when they 'look upon the one whom they have pierced'.[3]

But in this poem eternity is much closer to hand than Calvary. Mandelstam elides heaven with memory in moments that are

---

2 Psalm 36.9 (Coverdale).
3 Zechariah 12.10; 13.1.

both fleeting and endless, 'an instant of splendour', that 'little meadow where time does not flow', an 'eternal noon'. These phrases brighten into visibility a desire that is both joy and mourning. The complex, ambivalently personal wistfulness of Patricia Lockwood's description of a memory – 'up rises that round image of the bread through the glass – bread that my own father had consecrated'– also speaks from Mandelstam's poem in an intense and undefended form.

Yet, as with Lockwood's image, Mandelstam's seeing also 'spreads' beyond the flat, seen image into a strong sense of the nourishment of presence. Sight and participation blend. 'All partake of it, everyone plays and sings' writes Mandelstam. 'What happened enters into the house of what is always happening, and sits with it together, and eats at its table', writes Lockwood. Visual as it is, Mandelstam's poem is not distanced. Its looking is deeply embodied, deeply collective, working profound physical changes upon those who watch.

Flat eucharist

I've called this chapter 'Flat Eucharist'. It's 'flat' because it thinks about the eucharist in two dimensions. In fact, it thinks about two different kinds of two-dimensional eucharist. One is textual; the other visual. I've called the textual one 'schemes' and the visual one – for reasons obvious to any eucharistic participant who has lived through pandemic times – 'screens'.

Yet the screened eucharist is not just an issue for a passing historical moment. The nature of reality and presence for our three-dimensional humanity in the image-dominant digital world – that's an issue across all forms of human encounter. Thinking about eucharistic presence in its digital form casts an estranging light both on secular assumptions of the reality (or not) of screen encounter, and on sacred assumptions of the conditions for sacramental efficacy.

'Ordinary' eucharist – the kind celebrated physically and collectively in shared time and space – has at its centre a presence-in-absence, Jesus. That presence-in-absence, the reality of Jesus at the heart of the eucharist, is what underpins and yet splits apart our collective understanding of what, within the rite, counts as 'real'. When the eucharist is moved onscreen, so that space (and perhaps time) are no longer shared between its participants, the terms both of the absence and of the presence are disrupted. Sidestepping as it does the constraints of time and space to appear within a variety of discrete individual privacies, arriving upon the eye as flat and separated as the little unleavened discs of eucharistic bread: where, in a screened eucharist, is the reality of the Body?

Is it a 'flat' experience to see with the eye what cannot be apprehended in other ways? The thoughtful reader may wonder, for example, whether 'flat' is a very good description for the intense, participatory seeing of Mandelstam's poem of adoration. In Mandelstam's poem, as in Lockwood's description of the monstrance, text is powerfully employed to awake an inner encounter, to realize experience received through the eye. And there are longstanding traditions, pre-dating the pandemic by many hundreds of years, and existing in Western as well as Eastern Christianity, that privilege the bodily faculty of sight (rather than those of touch and taste) for participation in the eucharist. Adoration is action. Were looking a completely neutral activity, there would be no iconoclasm.

Sensual apprehensions

In the post-Reformation West, though – where iconoclasm was certainly felt necessary – sight has tended to be servant to touch and taste. Touch and taste must interact directly and very locally with our flesh, but seeing brings the distant (whether that distance is very small, or, with the aid of technology, very great) to act directly upon the mind. Sight is treated with suspicion and kept subordinate exactly because it is too powerful a faculty, implicitly promising to deliver knowledge above and beyond the immediately physical. We speak and think of sight in a curiously un-bodied way, as if it delivered to us imagined, non-empirical phenomena. This might mean that sight offered a particularly compelling experience of the real – the meta-real, as it were. Verbs of seeing and verbs of knowing blend in Greek and Hebrew as well as in English; sight and blindness are frequently used by Jesus as metaphors for truth and deceit.[4] Or it might, by contrast, mean that the interpretive variation for seeing's cognitive process renders it particularly untrustworthy: what is seen can always be potentially distinct from what is the case. 'Keep looking, but do not understand', says God to his people through Isaiah; and Elisha, in the second book of Kings, plays games of sight and blindness with the besieging Arameans, at the centre of which is the revelation of a formerly invisible divine host: 'So the Lord opened the eyes of [Elisha's] servant, and he saw; the mountain was full of horses and chariots of fire.'[5]

Touch and taste, on the other hand, are both means to simple truth. Thomas is invited to touch the risen Lord's damaged hands and to plunge his fist into the wound in his side: the invitation compels him to know that Jesus is alive, present and real.[6] The 'piece of broiled fish' that Jesus eats in the upper room, the fish he grills and serves to his friends in the early morning on a Galilean beach: these are earnests of a true and resurrected presence.[7] Sight alone might denote a ghost. Judas's betrayal is marked with a taste – bread dipped in sauce – and the touch of a kiss.[8] Neither sense deceives – even though the kiss is intended as an act of deceit Jesus is not fooled for a moment.

The slippery, double-edged nature of sight as a form of knowledge is exacerbated by the primacy of the textual in the print culture that shaped modernity. For the reformed sensibility, the power of sight is a swift route to idolatry. The making of images – the representation of forms within the world – carries

---

4 Matthew 13.13–17; Matthew 23.16–22; John 9.35–41; John 12.40.
5 Isaiah 6.9; 2 Kings 6.8–19 (quoted v. 17).
6 John 20.24–29.
7 Luke 24.36–43; John 21.9–14.
8 John 13.21–26, Luke 22.47–48.

the dangers of mistaking creature for creator, of ignoring the invisible God. Across the scriptures of the Old Testament, trust in the invisible, unreplicable creator is an act of faith and courage running counter to the fearful temptation to imitate, and then to worship, what may be seen. 'Thus they turned their glory into the similitude of a calf that eateth hay' mourns the psalmist, pondering the Israelites' act of idolatry in making a golden calf as they waited for their absent God and his absent emissary, Moses, at the foot of Mount Sinai over many empty nights.[9]

The sixteenth-century reformers (like iconoclasts before them in earlier centuries) took the point. Representation – the world in miniature constructed by human ingenuity, whether that meant theatre, art, sculpture or a represented image of a faraway real place (as it might be onscreen, had they known of screens) – invited the present danger of idolatrous acts of seeing. And while these idolatrous acts were not inevitable, they were deeply feared. Images commanded a worship that properly belonged only to the invisible Godhead. Therefore – regardless of the accuracy or beauty of their imitation of the world's real things – they deceived.

For the Reformers, text was another matter. The scriptural Word (and the rise of the new technology of the printing press was bound tightly to the dissemination of that scriptural Word, quickly though it would branch out) was a place to discover a truth even more reliable than direct experience. For Luther, as we have seen, the authority of the scriptural Word could transform the physicality of bread into the mysterious, unseen, but even more real, physicality of Christ's body. It was its own *daronositsa* – the rite of eucharist obeyed a command, 'do this in remembrance of me', that also existed within the rite itself as a speech-act. It conveyed the Host, and it was the Host. None of it could work without the authority of the scriptural text, the divine command: 'take; eat; this is my body'.

---

9 Psalm 106.20; Exodus 32.

Fractured attention

One practical outworking of the history of eucharistic worship in the post-Reformation West, then, is that the different sensual modes of conveying the sacred are actually in competition. Text – with its requirement of translation for inner realization – and the outward worshipping gaze do not exist well together. Within the eucharistic rite they jostle against each other, trying to do similar work by different means – not just in the philosophical collision of word versus the slipperiness of the sensual, but in a simple division of attention. Even during in-person worship, the worshipper at a eucharistic service must choose whether to 'follow the script' (gazing at a printed or screened text) or to lift their eyes to the action: they cannot do both. Yet the text – often a scriptural mélange rearranged for transformatory performance – is the reformed worshipper's guarantee of a textual truth more authentic than the evidence of the senses. In this way the fracture in our history of eucharistic devotion replicates itself in a fractured attention during worship.

Here is a striking example of how paralysing this could be devotionally. The Protestant martyrologist John Foxe, in his Good Friday sermon at St Paul's Cross in 1570, found visual images so dangerous that he refused to realize the crucifixion pictorially at all. Rather than Christ's actual body upon the cross, he asked his hearers instead to imagine, nailed to that cross, the legal text of humankind's transgressions as described in the second chapter of the letter to the Colossians (2.14). This is not just a historical curiosity: Foxe has his inheritors. Enter the Colossians text into a search engine and you will find a multitude of images showing a cross with the words nailed to it instead of a physical body.[10]

---

10 John Foxe, *A Sermon of Christ Crucified, Preached at Paules Cross* (London, 1570), fos.53r–54v, quoting Colossians 2.13b–14: 'God made you alive together with him, when he forgave us all our trespasses, erasing the record that stood against us with its legal demands. He set this aside, nailing it to the cross.' See, for example, https://www.pinterest.

If visualizing the cross was a problem (and it was), visualizing the eucharist was infinitely worse. No Christian – well, almost no Christian, barring a few laggard Docetists – was going to argue whether the cross held the body of Christ or not: it did. On the other hand, there really was a massive issue about whether the eucharistic elements held Christ's body. And in terms of late medieval devotion, that body was largely apprehended through sight. The theologian David Grumett speaks of 'the distant view of the white host elevated by the priest above his head to be seen by the people from behind, often against a dark-coloured curtain, comprising the literal high point of their merely visual participation'.[11]

Gadding, gazing

No surprise, then, that visual eucharistic adoration was a prime target for reformers anxious about idolatry. Here is Thomas Cranmer, writing on the eucharist in the late 1540s, in vividly hostile mode:

What made the people to run from their seats to the altar, and from altar to altar, and from sacring (as they called it) to sacring, peeping, tooting and gazing at that thing which the priest held up in his hands, if they thought not to honour the thing which they saw? What moved the priests to lift up the sacrament so high over their heads? Or the people to say to the priest, 'Hold up! Hold up!'; or one man to say to another 'Stoop down before'; or to say 'This day have I seen my Maker'; and 'I cannot be quiet except I see my Maker once a day'? What was the cause of all these, and that as well the priest and the people so devoutly did knock and kneel at

---

co.uk/pin/nailed-to-the-cross-colossians-214--390124386453098876/ (accessed 13.2.2023).

11 David Grumett, *Material Eucharist* (Oxford University Press, 2016), p. 9.

every sight of the sacrament, but that they worshipped that visible thing which they saw with their eyes and took it for very God?[12]

When Cranmer came to construct the communion service in English, in its first iteration of 1549, his rubric at the consecration of the bread was explicit: 'these wordes before rehersed are to be saied, turning still to the Altar, without any elevacion, or shewing the Sacrament to the people'.[13]

Cranmer's point, of course, was that you couldn't allow elevation, or turn west to face the people to make the host more visible, because congregations were adoring the wrong thing. They were mistaking the creature of bread for its divine creator – a creator who could not be detected in a single atom of the bread's physical being, and yet who in the course of the ritual would transform the believing heart. For Cranmer, slightly counter-intuitively, the move from visual adoration to the physical reception of bread and wine corrected the worshipper's focus from outward contingent physicalities to inward truths. 'There is *nothing* really and corporally in the bread to *be* worshipped', he remarked, off the back of an argument of Augustine's that 'Christ is not otherwise to be eaten than spiritually.'

And so, therefore, the unreformed church, those 'papists' as he called them, had got it all wrong.

Why do they run from place to place to gaze at the things which they see, if they worship them not? ... Why do they not rather quietly sit still in their seats, and move the people to do the like, worshipping God in heart and in spirit, than to gad

12 Thomas Cranmer, *A Defence of the True and Catholic Doctrine of the Sacrament of the Body and Blood of our Lord Jesus Christ* (London, 1550). Here quoted in the online edition of 1825: https://archive.org/details/defenceoftruecat1825cran/page/226/mode/2up (accessed 13.2.2023).

13 *The Book of Common Prayer: the Texts of 1549, 1559, and 1662*, ed. Cummings, p. 31.

about from place to place, to see that thing which they confess themselves is not to be worshipped?[14]

Cranmer writes in this way because he assumes that to 'gad about' in order to 'see' a physical object can only be an idolatrous act – even, or perhaps especially, if the object to be seen performs a sacred function. His logic seems to be that seeing always tends towards a dangerous adoration – you would only 'run from place to place to gaze' if you were worshipping the thing that you travelled to gaze upon. (What, I wonder, would the pilgrimage-hating Cranmer make of the modern tourist industry?) To meet God all one needs to do is to 'quietly sit still' and turn the heart inwards to the invisible deity. More than a hundred years later the poet Henry Vaughan would make the point more deeply and generously in his poem 'The Search', in which the speaker travels to the Holy Land seeking Christ and fails to find him, because he is only to be found within the worshipping spirit. Vaughan concludes his poem with three spare stanzas, very unlike the long lines of the rest of the verse, full of significantly empty space in its physical *mise-en-page*:

> Leave, leave thy gadding thoughts;
>> Who pores
>> and spies
> Still out of Doores,
>> descries
>> within them nought.
>
> The skinne, and shell of things
>> though faire,
> Are not thy wish, nor pray'r ...

---

14 Thomas Cranmer, *A Defence of the True and Catholic Doctrine of the Sacrament of the Body and Blood of our Lord Jesus Christ* (London, 1550). Here quoted in the online edition of 1825: https://archive. org/details/defenceoftruecat1825cran/page/226/mode/2up (accessed 13.2.2023). My emphasis.

Search well another world; who studies this,
Travels in Clouds, seeks *Manna*, where none is.[15]

It's striking that Vaughan reaches for the same verb as Cranmer
for vain physical searching: 'gad'. Its primary meaning 'to travel'
has a secondary implication of losing one's way, wandering
from the true path.[16] The reformed sensibilities of these two
men do not allow them to see anything sacred in the material
stuff of this world's life: to adore the Host is to '[seek] Manna,
where none is'. The spiritual food of Christ's presence comes
to humanity beyond the boundaries of the physical – 'Search
well another world' – and to follow one's desires in this one is
to stray.

During the years of the pandemic, physical 'gadding' wasn't
available; nor, for much of that first year, was the material stuff
of communion bread. Staying at home, most worshippers had
to meet the sacrament by sight only, because for months on end
its physical reception was forbidden. Seeing the Host blessed,
broken and consumed at an onscreen eucharist was the closest
many got to 'partaking'. In some ways the experience of eucharist at the height of the pandemic was more like the experience
of an Ignatian meditation, with the sounds and images on the
screen acting as prompts to inward imaginative attention.

Really present?

There are some ironies here. Those modern Christians most at
ease with the gaze that went with online eucharists were, on
the whole, Cranmer's inheritors, because it was those surest
that 'Christ is not otherwise to be eaten than spiritually' who
were least troubled by receiving no material, consecrated bread.
Research conducted then about online eucharists discovered,

---

15 Henry Vaughan, *The Complete Poems*, ed. Alan Rudrum (Penguin, 1976), pp. 157–9.
16 *OED* (1989), 'Gad' v.2 (1 and 2).

for example, that, in the Church of England, evangelicals were far more comfortable with eating unconsecrated bread at home in front of their screens than catholic Anglicans were. After all, if the action of eating bread were only a prompt towards an inward event, it hardly mattered what bread was used or what had happened to it first.[17]

Ely Cathedral (along with a number of other churches that livestreamed their services) would put up, at the point of receiving the Host, a prayer by the eighteenth-century Catholic St Alphonsus Liguori, for the watcher to say. This prayer, unsurprisingly, pushes against that reformed tendency. It affirms 'I believe that You are present in the Blessed Sacrament' and following from that affirmation adds ' since I cannot now receive You sacramentally, come at least spiritually into my heart'. It is, therefore, explicit that this is only for times when receiving the sacrament physically is actually impossible – but much less explicit about what has actually *happened* to the devotional watcher as a consequence of making this 'spiritual' invitation to Christ.[18] (The Cathedral, post-pandemic, continues to put the words up for every livestream, on the charitable assumption that those watching are genuinely unable to attend in person.)

As the pandemic passed, priests and people worried and wondered about what exactly they thought they were doing in offering virtual eucharistic worship. Priestly responses ranged

---

17 Survey findings of Leslie Francis and Andrew Village, 'Covid-19 and Churches', in the *Church Times*, 19 March 2021 as 'Eucharist in a Time of Lockdown'. See https://www.churchtimes.co.uk/articles/ 2021/19-march/comment/opinion/eucharist-in-a-time-of-lockdown (accessed 13.2.2023).

18 Anecdotally, every comment that has come to me from worshippers on the nature of this prayer has been dissatisfied with it as a spiritual resource. This has been for a variety of reasons, from its 'sentimentality' to its clear affirmation of the Real Presence, to the ambiguity, as a *sacramental* event, of its invitation for Christ to 'come at least spiritually into my heart'. It might be said that it is really there not so much as a devotional aid as rather a kind of doctrinal insurance policy, for it both affirms a particular view on the sacrament and limits the claims that can be made for its livestreamed or recorded experience.

from the wholly easy welcome given to online communion by the Anglican priest and academic Richard Burridge in his (theologically careful but digitally naive) book *Holy Communion in Contagious Times*, to a very much more troubled response articulated in, for example, an article by Anthony R. Lusvardi, SJ, entitled 'We should stop filming the liturgy of the Eucharist'.[19] Lusvardi, who in 2020 was ministering in an 'unofficial Native American parish' in Rapid City, South Dakota, begins with the refusal of his Lakota elders to allow a Lakota penitential ritual, incorporated within the Mass, to be filmed along with the rest of the service. Why not, people ask. 'It's sacred. It's not a show.'

From here, Fr Lusvardi draws out his own unease with a 'staged' eucharist for the camera – a theatrical event to be performed on Wednesday for later, solitary, virtual consumption on Sunday. Some of his worry was about that shift to theatre; at least as much it was about losing the physical gathering of the community in shared time and space. 'Physical participation is what separates the sacrament from a pious wish', he writes – a perception very far from Vaughan's view that the pious wish trumps the 'skinne, and shell of things' every time.

Lusvardi also makes the point that not-seeing, or restricted seeing, are markers of the sacred too; as in the separation in the early Church's rites of Eucharist between the service of the Word and the reception of the Sacrament for initiates only, in a different room. His sense of the boundaries that must mark the sacred is in dramatic contrast to a conversation I witnessed at about the same time. In a national online meeting of Anglican Cathedral clergy one speaker, to general acclaim, said how marvellous it was that people could participate in the eucharist while at home in the bath. Lusvardi, in contrast, concludes that

---

19 Richard A. Burridge, *Holy Communion in Contagious Times: Celebrating the Eucharist in the Everyday and Online Worlds* (Wipf & Stock, 2022); Anthony R. Lusvardi, SJ, 'We should stop filming the liturgy of the Eucharist', see https://www.americamagazine.org/ faith/2020/11/24/livestream-mass-liturgy-coronavirus-stop (accessed 13.2.2023).

'our way of worshipping needs to testify more clearly to the fact that some things cannot go virtual. The Real Presence seems a good place to start.'

It is, of course, no surprise that a theology of real presence aligns with an unease about virtual communion.[20] And there is also no denying that online eucharists are both primarily visual and primarily solitary experiences – which also pushes uncomfortably against any vision, reformed or catholic, of a community united through communal eating and communal memory, participating in the same place and at the same time. Online participation brought people as close together as they were allowed to be, but whether what was experienced – perhaps in completely different time zones, and not in space at all – could be called 'presence' is difficult to say. The wave of depression sweeping the world in the wake of continued lockdowns suggests that virtual encounter, while better than total isolation, does not satisfy. We seem to need to bump up our this-world skins and shells against other people's more than we knew.

Also, more or less by accident, through online eucharists the Church of England, along with churches all over the world, entered a consumer market that positively encouraged a virtual version of 'gad[ding] from place to place'. Why go to your poorly resourced parish Zoom service when you could log in to the livestream at St Paul's Cathedral, or visit the magnificence of Washington DC?[21] At the same time, though, the proliferation of online eucharists broke through barriers that physical eucharists could not overcome. The curious watcher

---

20 It seems important to observe that most of the comments on Lusvardi's article, especially those from lay people, also of course Catholic, are very distressed and even angry at the thought of having the livestreamed sacrament withdrawn during the pandemic.

21 Again, that said, it seems important to acknowledge that several Ely Cathedral congregants, in conversation, have revealed casually that they would only regard watching the livestream of churches they usually attend in person as being 'real' participation. For them, it's about finding ways to be with a community to which they already belong.

could 'peep ... and gaze' without running the gauntlet of other inquisitive eyes, effusively terrifying welcomes, or complaints about whose seat they had accidentally sat in. Online euchar- istic visitors could sit in their pyjamas and look at the weird things Christians do, and not a soul would know. They could stop watching whenever they liked.

All the ritual's borders – whether good or bad – are down in online eucharist: place, time, even duration and order. The spectator can be as involved, or as casual, as they want, can hop from 'sacring to sacring' without moving from the kitchen table. The highly vexed question of whether the – possibly unbaptized, possibly unbelieving – visitor should receive never arises online in the way it does in person; they don't have to declare to be 'in' or 'out' of the eucharistic circle. They, like everyone else, are both there and not-there. Are they pilgrims or are they tourists? Is it a meaningful distinction? No one knows.

There that year, as well as the visitors, the seekers and the curious, were the faithful, looking for a way to affirm their corporate part, their participation in the Body of Christ. What were we, who believe and call ourselves Christians, understand- ing ourselves to be doing when we switched on our computers for the livestream or logged into the Zoom? Were we watch- ing other people receive, or was there some way in which we ourselves were receiving, parted as we were by distance, and perhaps even by time, present only through the eye? Is seeing something an act, or not, real or not-real? Could we say that we had been with others, when we had been sitting in a room alone looking at a screen?

Speaking casually with congregation members, often some- one would say 'I watched the eucharist', or 'I switched on the eucharist', and then stumble and correct themselves, perhaps to say they 'went online', perhaps by simply saying 'I don't know what words to use.'

During the second lockdown, once clergy were allowed back into their church buildings, the Zoom option was left open for our early morning eucharist at Ely Cathedral, so that those who had logged on for Morning Prayer by Zoom could stay, muted and invisible, but seeing. One of those cold dark mornings, in the huge space of the Cathedral and surrounded by the curious psychic silence of no physical congregation, as I raised the Host at the consecration in the sight of the computer, I found myself thinking, 'It's come full circle. It might as well be 1521, but the rood screen is electronic.'

Sex and sacrament

What kind of participation *is* online participation, especially for a service of the eucharist? Eucharist is a rite of presence but also of absence, of communal worship but also of personal devotion, of memory but also of the present moment, of material but also spiritual encounter with the divine. As with online sex, with which it has some unsettling parallels, we don't really seem to know how its simulations of presence sit in relation to – well – *real* presence. For, both in online communion and online sex, something that in the three-dimensional world would be an act of powerful significance, subsists much more ambiguously in the two-dimensional one.

This is vitally important not only for 'contagious times', but for our own, post-pandemic times, the world in which we live. We live in a culture where virtual presence is ordinary within private lives, within the world of work, and within the large domains of entertainment and leisure. All this happens via an online medium that is not a transparent, neutral means for access to experience that would otherwise be remote or inaccessible, but something much more loaded. I want, therefore, to think a little about what kind of experience online experience is for those encounters that have at their heart a physical event that meets and interacts with an Other – holy communion, and sex.

For communion – offline – we are physical because we eat together. For sex – offline – we are physical because one body meets and touches another body. For both, the irreducible element is corporeal; and for both, the curious thing is that although the framing goes on being one of corporeal encounter, online there is, at least where the watching is done, only one body physically present. So can the act retain its meaning without touch or taste – with only the physical faculties of sight and hearing as portals to bodily meeting?[22] And, if it can, how does that come about?

Sex and sacrament both have ritual rules of engagement, action-patterns that guarantee that the event is what it is. While these ritual rules have some fluidity, each has core elements without which the event has to be called something else. Communion is assisted by the clearer boundaries of an explicit liturgy, where particular words and motions are required for eucharist to be eucharist: the words of institution, the taking, blessing and breaking of bread, the priest's consumption of the bread and so on. There is no absolute consensus about where exactly the line between eucharist and non-eucharist lies – can a eucharist be a eucharist without a priest? Without certain actions? Without another participant besides the priest? But it's agreed that there *are* lines, even if they are drawn differently across denominations and traditions. This makes it a more stable field of meaning than what might count as 'sex', where for a few it will only mean penetration, for others orgasm, for others arousal according to particular forms, for others simple looking. What 'counts' as sex (and its close companion, consent) is both confusingly variable and unagreed. This is particularly tricky for sexual expressions that happen virtually.

---

22 Experiments in virtual reality, which attempt to bring an online experience to the physical body spatially (and may also experiment with other senses, such as smell and touch) are not currently trying to 'translate' an experience defined as 'real', but to provide a spectacularly convincing illusion. It may become a medium for 'real' experience one day, but does not do so now – so I leave it out of this argument. There have been films that play with the idea of VR as something approaching a genuinely alternative reality: for example the 2018 film *Ready Player One*; but *Ready Player One* is very clear that overlaying the physical world with a sensually convincing illusion is a dystopian idea, even as it invites watchers to be enchanted by its spectacular VR vistas.

Because online versions of these events are taking place without the apparently vital condition of physical presence, it's difficult to determine what quality guarantees their 'reality'. Does virtual sex, or virtual sacrament, qualify as an event at all – or is it a reflection of an event? Yet it seems to me quite significant that people do, in certain circumstances, define online versions of both sex and sacrament as in some sense 'real'. They neither of them belong to the category of a fully fictive experience – they both attempt to translate a reality across the divide.

Of course, communion, online or in person, never offers an absolutely unmediated presence – presence is always conveyed through the rite. So one way of understanding the eucharist's online 'reality' might be to appeal to its performative nature in the sense that J. L. Austin defined performative utterance (the 'speech-act'): particular words, in a particular context, accompanied by particular actions, simply do make something happen. In which case the only task in relation to the eucharist is to determine whether its online version has met sufficient minimal conditions for performative efficacy beyond the space and time of its performance.[23] Job done, no?

The heart has its reasons

If, that is, you believe that *actions* are the core of the event's reality at all. It's a small step from Cranmer's 'There is nothing really and corporeally in the bread to be worshipped ... Christ is not otherwise to be eaten than spiritually', to the locating of eucharistic efficacy solely in the heart's disposition. And is sex so different? Milton, that ingenious reformed thinker, was perhaps the first to argue, in his 1641 pamphlet *The Doctrine and Discipline of Divorce*, the theological case that the heart's joining outweighed in efficacy the body's sexual encounter:

---

23 J. L. Austin, *How to Do Things with Words* (Harvard University Press, 1962), p. 26: 'There must exist an accepted conventional procedure having a certain conventional effect, the procedure to include the uttering of certain words by certain persons in certain circumstances.'

[if] it were so needfull before the fall, when man was much more perfect in himselfe, how much more is it needfull now against all the sorrows and casualties of this life to have an intimate and speaking help, a ready and reviving associate in marriage; wherof who misses by chancing on a mute and spiritless mate, remains more alone then before, and in a burning lesse to be contain'd then that which is fleshly and more to be consider'd; as being more deeply rooted even in the faultless innocence of nature. As for that other burning, which is but as it were the venom of a lusty and over-abounding concoction, strict life and labour, with the abatement of a full diet may keep that low and obedient enough: but this pure and more inbred desire of joyning to it selfe in conjugall fellowship a fit conversing soul (which desire is properly call'd love) *is stronger then death*.[24]

From his argument that what made a marriage was the joining of souls rather than bodies would come, eventually, divorce on emotional rather than physical grounds, and its converse, the adulterer's reasoning that tells his (or her) partner an infidelity 'meant nothing'.

Absent hearts

Look at this the other way round, now. For sex in the material world, genuine emotional encounter of two selves alongside the physical act can be evaded by various means. It can be diluted by transaction, by paying for sex or entering some other kind of bargain about it; it can (in rape) be rejected with violence. In the online world, though, those choices – and their consequences – are not so clear. Online (I speak here of live interaction, not recorded porn), encounter is an elusive experience, because

---

24 John Milton, *The Doctrine and Discipline of Divorce* (1641), Book 1, chapter 4. See https://milton.host.dartmouth.edu/reading_room/ddd/book_1/text.shtml (accessed 13.2.2023).

the impact the other person will have upon the watcher is instantiated only in the responses of the watcher's own body. Physicality, by contrast, requires multiple sensory encounter – in touch, in taste, in hearing, in sight, in smell – to combine unpredictably as they arise in more than one physical body at a time. That unpredictability asks for a complex kind of mutual attention.

But mutual attention is difficult and risky, which is another reason why sex, too, is a ritual act with its own rules. In every kind of sexual meeting, whether physical or virtual, it's easier and safer to respond according to generic cues that regulate the balance of power than to pay over-close attention to self and other in the dance of encounter. The many cultural codes of sexual process act as public masks for the more diffident and involuntary responses of the private body, and those codes are what tend to blur the difference between real and virtual physical bonds. A mask is a mask. Once you have the rules of your personae, the particularity of the other participant is hidden, for their own defence as well as for yours; what happens behind the masks happens to the private person in a private and so a solitary way. Private satisfactions may stimulate memory or longing, but they are also very likely to remind the body that it is alone. In person, there might be something to challenge that reminder, even if it were unwelcome; online, there is nothing. So the paradox of the rituals of online sex is that, turned as they are towards the reliable arousal and response of the solitary body, they underline not encounter but loneliness.

For this reason, in all digital attempts towards it, the 'real presence' experience is actually very elusive. In online sacrament as in online sex, the watcher may conclude, at the end, that the Other they sought was no more than a chimera, an ephemeral set of internal brain-to-body responses. There is no 'real' meeting here to walk the heart into knowledge – heavenly or horrifying, transcendent or disappointed, all fade into the shadows from which they came.

So where is sacramental efficacy? And where is the unambiguous joining of the sexual act? It's as difficult, apparently, to dismiss the reality-status of online event as it is to confirm it. That helpfully consistent Catholic position on eucharist articulated by Fr Lusvardi looks convincing – until you notice what kinds of events it has robbed of meaning. There are those lay worshippers deprived of sacramental comfort if they cannot enter a physical building, and that's significant enough. But when you extend the principle to that other 'physical' activity, sex, a vast array of sexual behaviour is robbed of a power it very evidently possesses.

Eating up my people

Take the porn industry, for example – the internet's biggest sexual expression. It is highly reliant on maintaining a boundary between the fictive and the real, because its imaginings are so frequently violent.[25] For example: when 14-year-old Rose found the video online of her real rape by older men (under the tag 'teen getting destroyed') her challenge to the platform, Pornhub, was ignored until she had the bright idea of writing to them not as herself, but as a lawyer – at which point the platform took that video down. But it blended unnoticeably with the mass of other content similarly tagged: 'extreme teen abuse'; 'teen abused while sleeping'. When Pornhub was challenged about providing such content at all, it took refuge in the idea of representation as a form of thought: 'We allow all forms of sexual expression that follow our Terms of Use, and while some people may find these fantasies inappropriate, they

---

25 How frequent may be inferred from the 2022 discovery, by the UK's children's commissioner Rachel de Souza, of just how many children had access to pornography and what they concluded 'sex' to require from what they saw. That a 12-year-old boy should assume that kissing a girl should include semi-strangling her tells us a good deal about what 'mainstream' porn counts as a normal level of violence. 'Almost half of young people say girls expect sex to involve physical aggression, such as airway restriction,' the commissioner's report says. See https://www.bbc.co.uk/news/technology-64451984 (accessed 13.2.2023).

do appeal to many people around the world and are protected by various freedom of speech laws.'[26]

There are many, many Roses – and the boundary's permeability is also porn's great promise for its users. Imagining something *might* be true is the point – transforming or corrupting – of fantasy. For, at some level, all digital encounter piggybacks on the idea of having reality status, however deniable, and however useful that deniability might be for the purposes of consuming and abusing others. The practice of persuading children to perform sexual acts on themselves alone in their bedrooms, making videos that can then be sold on (a growing trend in abusive circles) attempts to throw all responsibility for the acts upon the children by pointing to the physical absence of any abuser. Look, no adult present – apart from those invisible watchers. It doubly traumatizes its victims by apportioning victim-blame while at the same time enhancing the reality status of the act, happening as it does in domestic settings that should have been safe.[27] It is difficult for police to act in such circumstances: no one is there to prosecute. The only visible person is the victim, an object tricked into imagining herself (99 per cent of victims are girls under 13) a subject.

What have these online cruelties to do with the holy eucharist? Why make these uncomfortable comparisons? What relationship could there be between what happens to innocent bodies caught in a cruel gaze and the gift of our crucified Lord? Innocent suffering and human greed have *everything* to do with the sacrament. Its liturgy re-enacts, in symbol and in narrative, the consumption of a body. And it does this out of a conviction that eating people is wrong. Deathly wrong. 'Their throat is an open sepulchre,' writes the psalmist of the wicked, 'eating up my people as it were bread.'[28]

---

26 https://www.bbc.co.uk/news/stories-51391981.

27 Report from the Internet Watch Foundation on *Woman's Hour*, Radio 4, 18 November 2022. See also www.iwf.org.uk (accessed 15.11.2022).

28 Psalms 14.4 and 53.4.

Jesus (who thought through the language of the psalms) said to his companions, 'Take; eat; this is my body.' He knew what he was doing when he asked people to eat him as if he were bread. His offer: Take me as a sacrifice, in exchange for every act of devouring the human race ever has or ever could make. Take, break and consume me, just as you take, break and consume each other in the commonplace voracity of the world, but learn that my ordinary act of sacrifice is of infinite value because I am also the infinite God. Devour me, in order to be freed of the appalling consequences of your devourings of each other. Eat me, to enter, however briefly, into a world where your needy emptiness no longer drives you to prey upon those around you, freed from the cruelty of your being by the constant gift of my self.

All this is also to say that the medium, while it may not *be* the message, cannot but alter the message. So it's not good enough to treat the online platform (as, for example, Richard Burridge does) as a fully transparent open window onto experience, as unambiguous in the nature of its seeing as the corporeal gaze of the human eye. That is not the truth of the online worlds that display themselves to us so invitingly. It does not describe the inexplicit transaction to which the seer finds she has assented simply by entering the portal. The 'free' model for internet encounter, based on the harvesting of customer data, was not an inevitable market model for online presence, but it has become so. It is the dominant mode for all non-physical encounter. And the point about it is that it requires the one who sees to be both consumer and consumed, without ever quite telling its users that the stuff of their lives is its ongoing and continual price. That is why a perfectly legal, highly successful global corporation can peddle the cruel and violent destruction of the young and the corruption of all whose desires are stirred by it, and call it business-as-usual.

And this medium – the speeded-up, logical end of a society based upon consumption – is the one into which we have decided to put a most sacred ritual at the centre of which is a body broken and consumed.

The Bread of the Presence?

I am not sure that we meant to place the holy eucharist inside the temple to the marketplace gods; but we did. The internet is a very strange platform upon which to choose to place the ritual that reverses all other greeds – but our sinful world was a very strange place for the incarnation, too. And it might be the boldest thing we could do – placing communion in the heart of all commodification, as God placed himself at the heart of our mortality. Or it could be extremely foolhardy. Are we blaspheming? Or are we, urgently hungry, sick of gobbling shadows, filling ourselves with the bread of the Presence – like David, risking the transgression in our need for nourishment?[29]

I don't know the answer. We took the eucharist online at a tricky time, for terribly practical, sensible reasons – and we are still doing it, because otherwise, in our world dominated by online representation, we feel our physical expressions to be ephemeral, powerless, invisible. If we are not on the internet, we think we are not really present at all. We are not just endowing online participation with the status of presence – we are sliding insensibly to finding eucharists that subsist online more real than the ones we failed to livestream or record. There's something terribly wrong about that.

Search well another world

The liturgical work of eucharist is to *realize* absence; we obey a command to remember someone who cannot be seen, heard, or touched with our physical senses. Eucharists are, then, always the work of the devotional imagination, always pointing elsewhere as well as happening here, whether online or in person.

---

29 See Exodus 25.30 for what the bread of the Presence is; 1 Samuel 21.1–6 for David's decision to eat it; Matthew 12.1–8; Mark 2.25–27; Luke 6.3–5 for Jesus's take on David's action.

The bread that we eat, is it not a sign of something so huge, so uncontainable, that it seems at times hardly there at all? Patricia Lockwood speaks with unsettling eloquence of the mixture of *nothing* and overwhelming *something* that communion evokes, as she describes one particular ordination day: 'I do not take communion, but the mere word brings the taste back to me. In childhood, we used to eat unblessed hosts by the fistful, not distinguishing much between them and my mother's Health Crisps.' She adds: 'They tasted like the second dimension ... ten seconds, and it would melt into nothing – no calories even, just a moment of texture.' A minute later, she is talking about sitting in empty churches to 'keep the eucharist company ... communing with an idea'.[30]

The mixture of nothing and something which is eating a communion wafer – 'the mere word brings the taste back to me' – and sitting in a church, no touch, no taste, no liturgy, but adjacent to the reserved sacrament, are, for her, closely similar experiences. She observes that she was essentially charmed by the way eucharist was metaphor, but leaves the reader wondering whether, or how, this really settles the whole issue of what the eucharist is or what it makes happen.

More than a metaphor

'Figures be called by the names of the things which they signify', Cranmer remarked.

> As a man's image is called a man, a lion's image a lion ... and likewise we were wont to say, Great St. Christopher of York or Lincoln; our lady smileth or rocketh her child, let us go in pilgrimage to St Peter at Rome ... which were not understood of the very things, but only of the images of them.[31]

30 Lockwood, *Priestdaddy*, p. 234.

31 Thomas Cranmer, *A Defence of the True and Catholic Doctrine of the Sacrament of the Body and Blood of our Lord Jesus Christ* (London, 1550). Here quoted in the online edition of 1825: https://archive.

He had a sophisticated understanding of signification as both connection and distinction. But he knew well enough that the balance between image as identity and image as difference wasn't very stable. If he had thought it was, he wouldn't have worried about visual adoration as much as he did. He would have trusted the people to find their devotion to the invisible God through something they could see. The ease with which Mandelstam, in the Orthodox tradition, could elide the bread that held Christ with the artefact that held the bread is, thanks to the anxiety of Cranmer and his inheritors, not something terribly available to the Western devotional sensibility. We worry when sign and signifier meet and kiss. Yet perhaps it is the only means by which screened, physically-distanced eucharists may give their gifts to us at all.

I confess I find Cranmer's anxious eagerness to disconnect sign from signifier depressing. When I think about people, ordinary people in, say, 1521, saying to each other, 'This day have I seen my Maker', or 'I cannot be quiet unless I see my Maker once a day', I feel nothing but sorrowful for a love that has so comprehensively, so successfully, been argued away. I remember the uniquely strange experience of sitting at my computer watching the unchanging, light-filled image of the reserved sacrament at 2020's online 'Watch of the Passion'. The intensity of it, image of an image, at a distance from me but with the sun declining at the same pace as it declined in the room where I was sitting at my screen, could hardly be borne.

When did you last only *listen* to a eucharist? I cannot ever remember one being broadcast solely on radio – though it has occasionally happened. To read a eucharistic script is, equally, not participation. However much we emphasize, and argue over, the power of the words of the rite, words remain servants to our bodily, sensual participation rather than standing free as a synecdoche (the metaphor that names the part for the whole) for the whole rite.

org/details/defenceoftruecat1825cran/page/218/mode/2up (accessed 13.2.2023).

Packet eucharist

The liturgical 'scripts' of service order are flat maps. It's only because those maps are linguistic that they are so privileged over sight and action. Language bounds, directs and channels experience, while sight and action are less easy to control. Language also preserves action that has happened across time: stuck on a desert island with a liturgical script, the castaway can reconstruct the sacred event like adding water to packet soup, though the relation of the eucharistic script to its reader may be different for the ordained and for the lay.

Cranmer's unease about visual adoration was very largely because he felt people couldn't be trusted, or known, to look in the right way. The problem with visual adoration, and indeed with all ritual action that isn't hedged with explanation, is that it's impossible either to police or to create boundaries. You just can't be confident that people will think the right things unless you tell them what the right things are. Once you have, and have recorded it in your liturgical script, you can ensure that they iterate right thinking over and over again until it has become their own habit of being. 'Religion trains you like roses', writes Patricia Lockwood.[32]

The screened eucharist, then, is remarkably *un*reformed in that its porous boundaries and visual emphasis allow it to slip freer of policed interpretation than the traditional in-person service. Though service sheets may be provided and watched on another screen, that split sensibility is often just too much, and since the watcher's response is likely not to be seen and certainly won't be heard, service orders become much less important. 'I love watching online', one Ely Cathedral congregation member confided. She added, 'I can sing in tongues as I watch. I don't think *that*' – with a hint of mischief in her voice – 'would work in person, would it?'

Of course, she's right. Textual schemes – even the textual schemes of praise – are about as different from singing in tongues

---

32 Patricia Lockwood, *Priestdaddy*, p. 234.

as anything could possibly be. A major liturgical task, linguistically, is to calm the fears of the Church of England's inner reformer by endlessly rebuilding the walls between orthodoxy and heterodoxy. Liturgy synthesizes and summarizes theological consensus (where possible) and so binds the worshipping community into an acceptable range of interpretations. We spend a lot of our worshipping time on an uneasy boundary between poetics and argument, between adoration and education.

And yet, some of that work is necessary. Our theological interpretation is plural, difficult to police, and largely a specialist activity rather than securely-possessed cultural knowledge. So liturgy is one of the few places where the faithful are schooled in the parameters of what they are trying to live. The *process* of eucharist, its devotional progression from praise to penitence to praise again, from listening and thinking to intercession to the expression of collective love, from the story of Christ's broken body to the affirmation of his living presence, from eating to thanksgiving, from receiving to going out in order to give – it's almost impossible to endure when you are angry, rebellious, or revengeful. It's too painful. In person, you can't run away: you are carried towards universal charity in spite of yourself.

Attention deficit

Online, who would know whether you bothered to try? The platform is set up to distract, not to focus, the attention. Someone who watches a 60-minute eucharistic service is behaving extremely counter-culturally on a platform that considers a 30-second view to be a very significant engagement.[33] A consumption-focused online experience wants to maximize engagement through the sheer number of experiences sampled in a given time. You are absolutely not inviting your viewer to concentrate. The whole point is to break that concentration, to ambush the attention.

---

33 An interesting exception to this trend is the rise of the long podcast.

The Marxist blogger Mark Fisher talked about the effect of this upon music production and tastes in a piece he wrote on retro styles in 2009. His observations have real significance for the worship experience, because they point out how *difficult* the sustained concentration that eucharistic worship demands is becoming for generations shaped in all its preoccupations (packaged music and packaged sex being the biggest activities of all for modernity) by the deliberate distractions of late capitalist culture. He writes:

> As [Franco] Berardi has argued, the intensity and precarious-ness of late capitalist work culture leaves people in a state where they are simultaneously exhausted and overstimulated. The combination of precarious work and digital communications leads to a besieging of attention. In this insomniac, inundated state, Berardi claims, culture becomes de-eroticized. The art of seduction takes too much time and, according to Berardi, something like Viagra answers not to a biological but a cultural deficit; desperately short of time, energy and attention, we demand quick fixes. Like pornography, another of Berardi's examples, retro offers the quick and easy promise of a minimal variation on an already familiar satisfaction.[34]

Whereof reason knows nothing

Even for those few who still know how to concentrate, our textual schemes, our privileging of right and intentional thinking, are problematic in worship. Worship is a space made for encounter with the divine; and experience, like God himself, is other than the language that describes, locates and limits it. The poet is more likely to recognize this truth than the liturgist,

---

34 Mark Fisher, 'The Slow Cancellation of the Future', in *Ghosts of My Life: Writings on Depression, Hauntology and Lost Futures* (Zero Books, 2014), p. 14. Franco Berardi, whom he quotes, is an Italian Marxist philosopher who works on the role of IT in late capitalist society.

especially if the liturgist is too preoccupied with the linear process of educating worshippers. I began with a poem for a reason.

Our liturgy is hammered out through a dialectical process – the point and counterpoint I talked about in the last chapter – which establishes consensus and compromise in our expression of the things of God. It is linear; it is discursive; it discovers what words can do, and it has less purchase – or only a negative purchase – on the things words *cannot* do.

A couple of examples. The so-called absolution in Cranmer's Matins and Evensong offices is a perfect example of a linguistic action qualified almost to extinction. Here it is in full:

> Almighty God, the Father of our Lord Jesus Christ, who desireth not the death of a sinner, but rather that he may turn from his wickedness, and live; and hath given power, and commandment, to his Ministers, to declare and pronounce to his people, being penitent, the Absolution and Remission of their sins: He pardoneth and absolveth all them that truly repent, and unfeignedly believe his holy Gospel. Wherefore let us beseech him to grant us true repentance, and his Holy Spirit, that those things may please him, which we do at this present; and that the rest of our life hereafter may be pure, and holy; so that at the last we may come to his eternal joy; through Jesus Christ our Lord. Amen.[35]

Behind this prevarication lies a sixteenth-century theological argument about the terms upon which absolution could be conferred at all. Although the intention of such a hedged pronouncement is to remind worshippers that God's forgiveness responded to their personal penitence rather than to the minister's actions, it also demonstrates deep scepticism about the efficacy of ritual gesture. This leaves penitents stuck with resolving all by themselves an inner war between regenerate and unregenerate impulses. The ritual has announced – at quite some length – that it can do nothing.

---

35 *Book of Common Prayer*, ed. Cummings (2013), p. 241.

Mea culpa

In modern liturgies, on the other hand, the human sense of sin has been deliberately moved away from personal and towards corporate responsibility. Nowadays, liturgies of confession are relatively uninterested in assisting us to repent of our personal failures of loving-kindness. Instead. we repent of the systemic, unwilled collusion we cannot help but live with simply by being part of human society at all. This sticks penitents with a different kind of helplessness, for even after the absolution has been conferred it's wholly unclear what, if anything, of the burden of general human wickedness has actually been lifted from our shoulders. We are still tied in with all that awfulness, too heavy to lift. Sometimes we really do just want to say, 'through *my own* fault, my own most grievous fault', and be released.

I am not just saying, look, here are some user-unfriendly decisions in liturgy. I'm not, even, just saying, look, theological arguments are games with experiential consequences for faithful Christians – though I *am* saying that too. I'm pointing out liturgical decisions that make liturgy powerless – and therefore redundant. Cranmer's worry about ritual efficacy leaves him with nothing but words. Modern acts of penitence place upon the shoulders of every worshipper – briefly, almost casually – the full inertia of a whole world of sin. Then they just move on. It's a short step from reminding Mrs Jones that she is personally responsible for the unshiftable weight of human evil, to finding that Mrs Jones has despaired of ever finding any freedom from the systemic sin she is implicated in and has given up penitence in favour of anti-depressants. Why go through a liturgy that piles it on and can't take it off?

Theological argument, while serious, is also a game and a career. You don't have to believe it to play it. It influences, but doesn't claim responsibility for, the lived-out work of the Christian life. It's another two-dimensional map, the often beautiful schematic patterning of Christian logic, rather than the three- and four-dimensional mess and complexity of flesh and blood, bones and breath and being.

Over the centuries, the distance between academic theology and personal, lived devotion has lurched backwards and forwards. The rise of religious houses happened as a corrective to the professional wrangling of university debate; and that uneasy relationship – sometimes close, sometimes distant – has been going on ever since.[36] We are a bit distant at the moment. Theology and devotion find it difficult to converse in ways that are not stilted, artificial or unequal. Our language for the things of God needs breath to vivify it. At the same time our array of modes for Christian *practice* are poverty-stricken. They are weirdly transactional, filled with aspartame instead of honey. You cannot feed the hungry soul just with a Jesus-shaped slogan.

Schemes and screens

What, then, have we learnt about the flat, two-dimensional planes of text and image? First, we have learnt that they are not talking well to each other. Perhaps more urgently, we have learnt that neither of them is well integrated into the three-dimensional world of experience, the world in which rituals bring about change. Words are not always actions. Seeing is not the same as presence. In screen and in scheme, we seem to stand alongside ourselves, wondering how we might ever be truly present before God.

The historian Miri Rubin, writing about late medieval eucharistic practice, argues that (in the words of David Grumett) 'the reification of spiritual presence produced a material absence in the Church's life'.[37] In other words, the imaginative work demanded of purely visual adoration was not enough. And yet the reformed legacy, playing out to this day in the life of *all* churches, including the Church of England, has its own even fiercer tendency

---

36 Justo L. Gonzalez, *The History of Theological Education* (Abingdon Press, 2015).

37 Miri Rubin, *Corpus Christi: the Eucharist in Late Medieval Culture* (Cambridge University Press, 1991), summarized in Grumett, *Material Eucharist* (Oxford University Press, 2016), p. 9.

to reify the internal, the imagined, the felt, and to dismiss the non-negotiable corporeal signs of presence: of space and bodies and place and time, of action and touch and taste.

In our internet-haunted world, fresh from a pandemic where each body represented a threat to all other bodies, we are forced to think hard and urgently about the value of real presence. Would anyone really wish to encounter a simulacrum of the person they love rather than the person themselves? Would they really choose to eat the bread that does not satisfy, if they could eat the bread of heaven?

When *shall* we come before the presence of God?

3

The Eucharist as Theatre: Place, Space and Bodies

That Holy Room

In – probably – the year 1623, John Donne, poet and priest, wrote verses about the work of dying. He was prompted to it by his own sickness and fever, from which he more than half-expected to die but didn't. Here are those verses:

Hymn to God my God in my sickness

Since I am coming to that holy room,
    Where, with thy choir of saints for evermore,
I shall be made thy music; as I come
    I tune the instrument here at the door,
    And what I must do then, think here before.

While my physicians by their love are grown
    Cosmographers, and I their map, who lie
Flat on this bed, that by them may be shown
    That this is my south-west discovery,
    Per fretum febris, by these straits to die,

I joy, that in these straits I see my west;
    For, though their currents yield return to none,
What shall my west hurt me? As west and east
    In all flat maps (and I am one) are one,
    So death doth touch the resurrection.

Is the Pacific Sea my home? Or are
    The eastern riches? Is Jerusalem?
Anyan, and Magellan, and Gibraltar,
    All straits, and none but straits, are ways to them,
    Whether where Japhet dwelt, or Cham, or Shem.

We think that Paradise and Calvary,
    Christ's cross, and Adam's tree, stood in one place;
Look, Lord, and find both Adams met in me;
    As the first Adam's sweat surrounds my face,
    May the last Adam's blood my soul embrace.

So, in his purple wrapp'd, receive me, Lord;
    By these his thorns, give me his other crown;
And as to others' souls I preach'd thy word,
    Be this my text, my sermon to mine own:
'Therefore that he may raise, the Lord throws down.'[1]

As Donne wrote, London was in the grip of infectious sickness; and Donne himself was in physical isolation ('Even the
Physician dares scarce come'), a difficult experience that he
also wrote about in a series of prose reflections, *Devotions on
Emergent Occasions*.[2]

He had, therefore, plenty of time to think, nothing but himself
to think with. The poem 'Hymn to God my God in my sickness'
represents the parameters of his dying self, a self of the body and
its perceptions. His metaphors of place play highly characteris-
tic games with size, boundaries and dimensions. Space and time
are malleable, but not separable. The speaker's bodily being is
a 'little World': a small sentient piece of earth with unbounded
imaginative reach – another image he developed at length in the

---

1 *John Donne: Complete Poetry and Selected Prose*, ed. John Hayward (The Nonesuch Press, 1929), pp. 320–1.

2 John Donne, *Devotions Upon Emergent Occasions and Several
Steps in my Sicknes* (London, 1624).

Devotions.[3] Here, confined and dying, this speaker nevertheless contains everything. Infinite divine vistas arise from mortal
limits – vistas as real, and realler, than anything the dying body
might immediately touch, see or feel.

His physical body 'flat on this bed', as still and as supine as
the blocks of words on the flat page, is also febrile and protean
in its constant change. So: he's sick, he's about to be turned into
pure sound, no, he's a map, no, he's toiling feverishly through a
confined and choppy channel, in fact, he's Magellan the adven-
turer or maybe he's the place Magellan sailed through, he's the
whole world, he's a sphere, he's a flat square – oh no, wait, he's
folded his square into a circle, making the edges meet, so pre-
sumably he's become some kind of cylinder – he's Adam, he's
Christ, he's upright, planted like a tree, like a cross, he's in the
pulpit, he's in the pew listening to himself, he's shamed, he's
royal, he's dead, he's alive, he's toppled flat, he'll stand.

Yes: it's a poem by Donne all right. The fierce, chunkily awkward orderliness of the grammar and versifying conceals, or
partly conceals, the hallucinatory tumble they hold in place.
The speaker's experience presents as physical spaces closely
resembling the dream landscapes of fever, where the body's
pain and discomfort assume concrete but changeable forms.
(It's tempting to wonder how much of Donne's adult life he
spent with a high temperature.)

For Donne, though, that heightened strangeness allows him
to picture, not illusion, but a different kind of real. Enfolded
in these physical places there is the unseen landscape of the
soul's journey to another country, far beyond the stars. Ferdi-
nand Magellan first named the Magellan strait the 'Strait of All
Saints' (*Estrecho de Todos los Santos*).[4] Donne's poem, turning
on a pun between 'strait' as narrow endurance and 'strait' as

---

3 'It is too little to *call Man a little World*: Except *God*, Man is a
diminutive to nothing', *Devotion* 4, in *John Donne: Complete Poetry
and Selected Prose*, ed. John Hayward (1929), p. 511.

4 See https://en.wikipedia.org/wiki/Strait_of_Magellan (accessed
13.2.2023).

sea-channel, translates that same perfectly real sea route into the narrows of the *ars moriendi*, the last arduous journey to physical dissolution undertaken by, yes, all saints.

And this is only the most new-fangled of his bits of sacred geography. Along with the 'discovered' vistas of hitherto unknown but real places, offered as metaphors for otherworldly revelation, here also are the ancient landscapes of faith. All undiscovered lands are the plantings of Noah's sons, Shem and Ham and Japhet, spread long ago at God's command to the ends of the wide earth. Jerusalem and its environs, city of spiritual home, appears again at different ends of God's chronology, as the ground – the same ground – for innocence and for redemption, for 'Paradise' and for 'Calvary'. Like the dying body containing it, the holy city is both primordial garden and a violently inscribed, deathly wasteland.

Donne isn't playing a clever game of spiritual fantasy football. Nor is this wordspinning in order to make himself feel better about his own potential extinction. He holds a view of reality very different from ours: the fractured epistemology of early modernity has made relatively few inroads upon his modes of knowing. Therefore he makes his poem out of metaphors that conceive material stuff, the stuff of world and physical body, to be holy. The reality of God inheres in embodied experience: real places, real flesh. Even the disorder of a feverish perception bespeaks God's presence.

Donne is therefore unlikely to fall into the common mistake of the modern consciousness. He won't be assuming bodily perception to be a completely reliable external picture of an insentient world. Such an assumption must also assume that all *unlikely* perceptions are incorrect deviations from the unchanging, predictable norm of the real. Donne does not have to think that. For him, the world and our bodily perceiving of it are in a counterpoint of mutual knowledge disclosing the unpredictable, the un-commandable, presence of God. He knows that the body's responses can deceive – he wrote a sermon insisting that those feeling physical terror in their final hours should not see that terror as a sign of God's abandonment. But he was not tempted as we are to confine God's power to that illusory construct, incorporeal thought.

The locational boundaries of Donne's sacred knowing, west for death and the setting sun, east for life and its rising, tell of God's unlocated, unbeginning, unending, timeless being. The flat square folds up into the eternity of the circle, as round as the round world it depicts, so that west and east touch: 'death doth touch the resurrection'. Eternity is as much more present than the mortal conceptions of space and time as the real round world is than the flat map that denotes it. Donne's body, the flat map in question, looks in this poem towards acquiring a third dimension.

Repeatable versions

In the previous chapter I considered the eucharist in linear form, as thought and argument; and in two-dimensional form as a flat object, apprehended by the eye. These are forms that can float free of the one-way, experiential movement of the world's time. In this chapter the eucharist comes into *place* – into bodies and actions – and so the world's time matters: the third dimension falls within the boundaries of duration.

I began with Donne's poem, though, because it is three-dimensional in a particular way, where bodily experience, physical place and historical time are the grounds for eternal transformation, of being 'changed ... in the twinkling of an eye'.[5] The poem is set at a real turning point between death and resurrection, within the experience of dying. Being a poem, and not itself a bodily event, this turning point is textually rendered, a repeatable picture of experience and not experience itself.

The sacrament of eucharist is also made out of bodily experience, physical place and experiential duration, in order to bring about eternal change. Like Donne's poem, but by different

---

5 1 Corinthians 15.51–52. This chapter is the set reading for the *Book of Common Prayer* Burial Service.

means, it provides a repeatable version of itself: of structure, words and action within a place. Each iteration of its repeatable form is both a transformation of its own, within time, space and bodies as we experience them now and here, *and* an anticipatory taste of eternal transformation in the hereafter, when repetition will no longer have to act as our stuttering imitation of endlessness. Receiving the eucharist is more solid, but also therefore more fleeting, than reading Donne's poem, because it happens to our bodies in time, much as love poetry and the act of love offer very differently constituted joys.

Signs and remnants

Our text-obsessed sensibility tends to see the eucharist as dominated by thought and word, but thought and word are servants to its manifestation as *event*. I've called it 'theatre', because theatre offers the closest analogy for its mixture of script with action and location. Theatre itself, of course, has its roots in the sacred, within and beyond Christianity.

Like theatre, eucharist needs location of some kind, but can be translated to multiple locations that may be very different. And, like theatre, the movable event may also contain, within its script and instructions, symbolic traces of the sacred place where the event was first performed. You don't have to see Sophocles in the theatre at Ephesus to see how the theatre at Ephesus shaped the drama of Sophocles. Nor do you have to know the ancient geography of Jerusalem to envisage either the Last Supper or the holy city of Revelation, the place of Christ's return. Yet that lost city's traces are all over the eucharist, some easier to see than others. Our eucharistic prayers reiterate the words and actions of Jesus in the upper room in Jerusalem on the night of his arrest, as reported in the synoptic gospels and in Paul's first letter to the church at Corinth. That's the bit that's easy to see. But in this emphasis on symbolic re-enactment there are also less obvious signs of the holy city.

According to Gregory Dix, the eucharist shifted the balance

of its emphasis from eschatological hope to historical re-enactment in the fourth century, at the point that the Church was embraced and publicly established by the Emperor Constantine. As this-worldly Christianity becomes safer for its believers, so Dix argues, Christians look back more, and forward less: they are comfortable to live within the historical events of the world. They are not expecting sudden death, but can instead choose public social life as a Christian without fear. In the process of establishing Christianity, the particular places of the Christian narrative of redemption acquire a public holiness. Constantine made it his business to sacralize the places of Jesus's passion and death, beautifying and building on them.[6] Cyril of Jerusalem, bishop during this transformation and a citizen of Jerusalem from childhood, saw the change as it took place. 'It was a garden where he was crucified', he writes. 'For though it has now been most highly adorned with royal gifts, yet formerly it was a garden, and the signs and remnants of this remain.'[7]

Sacred buildings make Jerusalem into a site of pilgrimage: indeed, the contested nature of its sacred soil repeats and repeats across modern global politics. Back in the fourth century, Cyril's renewed liturgy arises from the ritualized, physical retracing of the events of Holy Week, moving from numinous site to numinous site. The itinerary of worship across the city is recorded in the diary of a visiting nun, Egeria.[8] However, the liturgies that suit the commemoration of a place where Jesus really was are not very exportable to places where he really wasn't. Cyril's own lectures to those preparing for baptism tend to point towards the actual landscape of faith, because it's on his door-

---

6 Gregory Dix, 'The Sanctification of Time', in *The Shape of the Liturgy* (Dacre Press, 1945), pp.347–53; see also Jonathan Z. Smith, *To Take Place* (University of Chicago Press, 1992), pp. 87–95.

7 Cyril of Jerusalem, *Catechetical Lectures, XIV*, in *The Nicene and Post-Nicene Fathers*, vol. 7 (T&T Clark, 1996), p. 94, para. 5.

8 G. E. Gingras, *Egeria, Diary of a Pilgrimage* (Paulist Press, 1970); J. Z. Smith, pp. 87–95.

step: 'Seest thou this spot of Golgotha?' he asks his hearers.[9] He doesn't mean metaphorically: he means out of the window. They shout their assent.

But in order for the event of eucharist to keep its stability wherever it happens, you need a template that will go anywhere. The honouring of actual places within worship and the physical travelling between them have to acquire a symbolic form that can happen in every place, independent of the geography of Jerusalem. And to solve this, place is translated to time. The liturgy of Holy Week is a temporal form of a physical journey, travelling through days instead of streets, time instead of space. It's still a process that changes the pilgrim, but the *pro*cessing, or perhaps the pro*cessing*, happens differently.

Just as Donne's word 'before' in his line 'and what I must do then, think here before' denotes progression both in time (from dying to being dead) and space (hesitating in front of the door of heaven and then entering it), so liturgists make our soul's journey temporal as well as spatial. Space is a common metaphor for time, which makes it easy – and strangely unnoticeable. Yet, in a sense, every church on Maundy Thursday becomes the lost Jerusalem. A little later, in the sixth century, the chant of *vexilla regis prodeunt*, 'the royal banners forward go',[10] starts life as a processional, sung while a piece of the True Cross was carried in pomp from Tours to its resting place in a monastery in Poitiers. For those without a piece of the True Cross, the procession and its chant could be put into Holy Week devotions. The True Cross ceases to be physical; it becomes instead a liturgical imagining of the Cross, an inner realization of a vanished object.

---

9 Cyril of Jerusalem, *Catechetical Lectures*, XIII, in *The Nicene and Post-Nicene Fathers*, vol. 7 (T&T Clark, 1996), p. 88, para. 23.

10 https://en.wikipedia.org/wiki/vexilla_regis_prodeunt (accessed 13.2.2023).

Res et verba

Later reformers, looking back on the early history of the Church, go through phases of saying that the rot set in with Constantine, loading us down with big expensive buildings, the worship of material stuff, public life, Establishment and its corruptions, and the morally dubious exercise of political power. Before that, Christianity was innocent, short on possessions, didn't do idolatry, and everyone worshipped at home in a really lovely way. They never had to raise money to keep the church roof on, and understood that it was inner faith that mattered not the outward show of material things.

There's as much back-projection as truth in such constructions of the past. All organizations, big and small, are riven with the politics of power, and the New Testament makes it perfectly plain that the early Church was no exception. And if buildings and locations became particular sites of the sacred with Constantine, then the bones of saints and martyrs were doing a very similar job before that.[11] All through its history the Church has lurched between iconic and iconoclastic sensibilities, sometimes seeing material stuff like buildings and relics as a helpful incarnational anchoring, and sometimes violently rejecting them. Stuck in the centre of it all, the eucharist, rite of corporeal transformation, cracks down the middle with the strain.

Because, if we can't agree whether physical ritual is a way to God or an obstacle on that way, we also can't agree, at least not stably, under what conditions the performance of the eucharist is efficacious. Sacred action is performative, in the sense in which the philosopher J. L. Austin used the term in his

---

11 See Caroline Walker Bynum, *The Resurrection of the Body in Western Christianity, 200–1336* (Columbia University Press, 1995, revised and expanded 2017); Caroline Walker Bynum, *Fragmentation and Redemption: Essays on Gender and the Human Body in Medieval Religion* (Zone Books, 1991).

famous lectures, *How to Do Things with Words*.[12] There Austin argued that under certain contextual conditions, utterances could make things happen in the world – rather than simply reporting or describing happenings. The umpire who declares a ball to be 'out' in cricket was one of his examples; another example was a marriage vow; yet others were making a bet or ratifying a legal agreement. He was, however, very clear that every example required the conditions of its context. Outside the game of cricket, the umpire's words have no power; outside the marriage ceremony and its legal adjuncts there is no vow. In the majority of his cases, 'context' meant a three-dimensional, acted-out set of culturally-agreed practices.

Austin was interested in situations where performative utterances were not accepted by all participants – where there was no consensus about their binding nature. An example he gives is duelling, where if one person won't accept the effectiveness of the challenge there is nothing the other person can do about it. Our current public life is full of misfired performatives of this kind, but on a terrifyingly large scale. The extent to which both British and American political structures rely on agreed conventions of uttered performance alongside law has been dramatically demonstrated in, for example, the weakening of democratic systems consequent on Donald Trump's refusal to concede the 2020 election results in a presidential speech. In the UK, the governmental political chaos and leader-churn, its loss of global influence and squandering of financial confidence are all outworkings of Boris Johnson's carefree readiness to lie, publicly and blatantly, throughout his term in office. Although without serious social impact for the individuals breaking the system for their own ends, the outcomes for the system itself, and so for all within it, continue to propel us into more and more dangerous levels of social instability.

Both leaders were, and are, popular. They demonstrate that our society's cultural impatience with responsible public utter-

---

12 J. L. Austin, *How to Do Things with Words* (Harvard University Press, 1962).

ance makes us especially vulnerable to destructive division.[13] This is because division happens when ritually representative figures snap the cultural bonds of their own performatives in the pursuit of an immediate goal. To look a little further back, the Government's readiness to ignore the UN, and indeed to lie about its own findings, in order to prosecute a war with Iraq in 2003 has had the effects of permanently weakening the UN's influence while at the same time giving Russia a justification for ignoring international condemnation for its war on Ukraine.

Misfired performatives are, therefore, signs of an institution beginning to break. It may be significant that the word 'performative' in ordinary usage has shifted away from Austin's precise meaning. It now means speech treated as a theatrically fictive performance. This has happened just at the point where habitual demonstrative lying has become normalized within democracies.

Theatre and eucharist

Back in the 1590s, only a generation or so away from the definitive break between sign and thing that the Reformation ushered in, a playwright (there is no consensus about which one) wrote a 'True Crime' drama called *Arden of Faversham*, based on a real case of a wife and her lover murdering her husband.[14] More linguistically straightforward than many of its contem-

---

13 This runs alongside an obsessive general scrutiny of all public utterance via all kinds of media, on a scale so detailed and far-reaching that it has become more or less impossible for any public figure to escape condemnation on some moral ground or other. Faced with the continual, ubiquitous policing of all kinds of utterance, one popular reaction seems to have been to find some relief and release in the deliberately flamboyant liar, indifferent to every kind of moral judgement. In our current context, lying begins to look more like honesty than any attempt to conform.

14 *Arden of Faversham* (London, 1592), l.101. See https://www.guten berg.org/files/43440/43440-h/43440-h.htm (accessed 13.2.2023).

poraries, and with a good deal of theatrical action available to it, it nevertheless chose to centre its dramatic tension within a language game that asks whether an uttered promise is binding.

Early in the play the adulterous wife, Alice Arden, sets out her stall: 'Love is a God, and marriage is but words'. Her case depends on her hearers accepting that words may reflect what is so, but cannot make anything happen: divine power lies elsewhere than in what people may say in any context whatever. (It is, perhaps, not a coincidence that her argument is a neat template for most modern arguments in favour of adultery.) But her position, prominent though it is in the play's thought, is not its motor. The matter that propels Alice and her lover, Mosbie, towards murder is another (and one would have thought a less powerful) linguistically binding utterance. Mosbie has made an oath to stay away from Alice during her husband Thomas Arden's lifetime. Alice regards Mosbie's dilemma impatiently from within the wreckage of her own performative marriage vows, saying to him:

[S]hall an oath make thee forsake my love?
As if I have not sworn as much myself
And given my hand unto him in the church!
Tush, Mosbie; oaths are words, and words is wind,
And wind is mutable: then, I conclude,
'Tis childishness to stand upon an oath.[15]

Mosbie admires her argumentative skill – 'Well proved, Mistress Alice' – and indeed what she offers is a kind of syllogism, a form of logic much respected in Elizabethan rhetoric; but he is not convinced by it. 'I'll keep mine [oath] unbroken', he says. Yet since his oath only applies while her husband lives, he can become a murderer without breaking his word. The rest of the plot follows on from this piece of reasoning.[16]

---

15 *Arden of Faversham* (London, 1592), ll. 434–41.

16 I am indebted to Adam Seligman for an extremely helpful private correspondence during 2020 on the nature of oaths.

In the first few generations after the Reformation, theatrical space was embattled – neither securely fictive, nor ritually binding, with an all-too-recent sacred history in both the ecclesiastical theatre of the Mass and the street theatre of the mystery play.[17] Elizabethan, and indeed Jacobean, theatre, is notably secular, word-heavy, even word-drunk on its rapidly expanding English vernacular, performed in permeable space where audience and actors mingle their realities, so that even in purpose-built theatres there is little in the way of fourth-wall convention.

Yet it was a satirical commonplace that *ecclesiastical* performers (in delivering sermons, for example) were suspiciously actorly;[18] and that secular actors' fictive mimicking of the world was dangerously close to making real-world stuff happen and could hurt the commonwealth, from the simple undermining of public morality all the way to outright treason. Hence the ubiquitous censoring of theatrical texts.[19] Words, it seemed, could change reality even in a carefully fictive context, so that the imitation of action was always in danger of spilling over into being real event. One pro-theatrical commentator came astonishingly close to commending the ancient Roman practice of using condemned criminals as stage extras, so that theatrical fights could have fatal but edifying real-world outcomes.[20]

---

17 A lucid and influential treatment of this issue may be found in Sarah Beckwith, *Signifying God: Social Relation and Symbolic Act in the York Corpus Christi Plays* (University of Chicago Press, 2001).

18 Jessica Martin, 'Godly Prototypes', in *Walton's Lives: Conformist Commemorations and the Rise of Biography* (Oxford University Press, 2001), pp. 117–23.

19 Prominent contemporary examples appear in Philip Stubbes, *The Anatomie of Abuses* (London, 1584) and Stephen Gosson, *The Schoole of Abuse* (London, 1579), as well as in the history of plays banned and/or destroyed, for example Sir John Hayward's *Henry IV* (thought to commend the Essex uprising of 1601) and Thomas Nashe's banned and destroyed play *Isle of Dogs* (1597).

20 Thomas Heywood, in *Apology for Actors* (1612), writes, 'It was the manner of their Emperours, in those dayes, in their publicke Tragedies to choose out the fittest among such, as for capital offences were condemned to dye, and imploy them in such parts as were to be

To find this in a *defence* of the theatre is remarkable, and tells us something about the intertwined nature of state perform-ance (which was a religious mode) and its ambiguously fictive shadow side in the imitative arts.

Religious-political currents, as well as disease, regularly closed theatres: indeed, disease was a common metaphor for theatre's contribution to the sickness of the state. There was, at the same time, an intimate relationship between the rhetoric of the stage and that of the law court, both in the history of impersonation (someone pretending to be someone else, including the very charged issue of those that transgressed class or gender bound-aries) and in the proliferation of argumentative play and quibble through which some solid conclusion about the nature of the real world might – or might not – be reached.[21] Theatre, that is, flourished in the jagged new breach between sign and thing, but its vigour arose from the recent trauma of the fracture.[22] *Arden of Faversham* reworked a 'true' story that pondered the binding nature of a speech-act, and began with the gift of sequestered monastic lands to the doomed husband by the Crown – presum-ably because of the prevalent superstition that accepting stolen

kil'd in the Tragedy, which of themselues would make suit rather so to dye with resolution, and by the hands of such princely *Actors*, then otherwise to suffer a shamefull & most detestable end. And these were Tragedies naturally performed.' Heywood, *Apology* (London, 1612), Book 2 (pages unnumbered), see https://quod.lib.umich.edu/e/eebo/A03185.0001.001?rgn=main;view=fulltext (accessed 12.2.2023) .

21 See Subha Mukherji, *Law and Representation in Early Modern Drama* (Cambridge University Press, 2007).

22 So it is that Heywood, in an exposition of ancient Greek theatrical practice, finds himself drawing attention to the distinction between sign and thing in an aside about boys dressing as women onstage: 'These [Greeks] … thought euen in those dayes, that Action was the neerest way to plant vnderstanding in the hearts of the ignorant. Yea (but say some) you ought not to confound the habits of either sex, as to let your boyes weare the attires of virgins, &c. To which I answere: The Scrip-tures are not alwayes to be expounded meerely according to the letter: (for in such estate stands our mayne Sacramentall Controuersie) but they ought exactly to bee conferred with the purpose they handle'. Heywood, *Apology* (London, 1612), Book 1.

monastic lands for a secular purpose was to accept, along with them, an evil fate. It's thrilling and powerful, but not at all safe, to tread ground scattered with sacred fragments.

Words, words, words[23]

Long before we decided that words were not necessarily binding at all, we could not agree, in all good conscience, on what kind of bond they were. The sacramental arguments of the sixteenth century onwards were seismic, and the landscape never looked the same afterwards; but it was also only the latest and largest upheaval in a long history of opposed understandings as to how God might operate in the world. We have been living within the scattered signs and remnants of sacred meaning for centuries, living among baskets full of the broken pieces of Christ's body. The ground is littered with gifts we don't know how to handle.[24]

As eucharist is a ritual of breaking as well as making, it is no surprise that its own processes break as well as make. How may we, in our symbolic practice, maintain a stable balance between the violence of the broken body and the nourishment of Jesus as gift? Between the presence and absence of the body we honour; between the signs and remnants in historical report and the expectant glimpses of Christ's coming again; between the mortal bodies and actions of the ritual here and now, and the invisible, eternal past and future it instantiates; between the simple, helpless love of remembering and the world-changing power of re-making?

However, at the heart of our conflict over eucharistic performance lies our difficult relationship with its performatives.

---

23 William Shakespeare, *Hamlet* (1600), 2.2.189, New Cambridge Shakespeare, ed. Philip Edwards (1985).

24 Perhaps the most influential 'signs and remnants' reading of post-Christian Western culture is Alasdair MacIntyre, *After Virtue: A Study in Moral Theory* (University of Notre Dame Press, 1981), though his answer to the question he poses is Aristotle, not Jesus.

Within the wide arc of Christians for whom participating in a eucharist is significant, we have no consensus about what happens and how. In Anglicanism, a tradition that generously attempts to contain opposed epistemological convictions, we worry about looking too hard at the performative qualities of its ritual in case the whole edifice flies apart. We can make our sacrament of unity the site for fierce division, or we can keep the conditions of our performative utterance so vague that they might not be binding at all. We have chosen the latter.

So we have technical arguments on the nature of required gesture, or clothing, or what actual words would be the core performatives, but these arguments are now largely ignored. Historically, they were a source of actual schism. This wasn't because the people of the past were more unreasonable than modern people. It was because they took the ritual context for performatives more seriously than we do.

Then there are our internal or inter-church arguments, about whether only a priest can make the performative binding, and indeed about what category of person can be deemed to be a priest. These are arguments that are still extremely live, but even they can begin to have a technical, semi-redundant look to them in a Church where the Archbishop of Canterbury can choose to stand by during an outdoor eucharist, leaving the children around him to bless, consecrate and distribute the pitta and juice boxes that represent the bread and wine.[25] For many of those within his Church, that would be a beautiful *agape* meal, but not a eucharist. For others, it would, emphatically, be a eucharist, because the priest's actions *as priest* would not, for them, be the conditions making the performative do its work. Last of all, for our internal arguments, there is who receives: whether the table is 'open' or closed, and what kind of conditions will open a closed table for those on the outside. What is it to 'receive unworthily', to use the words of Paul?[26] No one knows.

---

25 At the Greenbelt Festival, 2019.
26 1 Corinthians 11.27.

Cracks let the light in?[27]

On the whole, within most forms of Anglicanism, there is a general assumption that 'the Holy Spirit will complete our ritual deficiencies, so why worry?' It's not like we do it ourselves, or even understand its mystery, they will say, so it won't matter if there are lots of cracks in how we understand it. Surely the cracks will let the light in? That is the spirit in which, in the wake of a pandemic, we understand how something can be a eucharist that we watch but at which we are not present, do not meet anyone else, make no audible sound, do not receive, and may be worshipping at a completely different time.

I do have quite a lot of sympathy with this 'cracks let the light in' view. Like most faithful people, I rely heavily on the mercy of God to supply our human deficiencies, in life as in worship. But I don't think this means we should be indifferent to those deficiencies, or ignore their consequences (for they do *have* consequences) or give up on attempting to mend (rather than to ignore) what is broken in how we worship and in how we live. When we are indifferent to ritual we dilute what it may give – to us, and to those who might ask us what we are doing and why we do it. Just as a game without rules ceases to be a game, a ritual without boundaries becomes something other than a ritual. God doesn't need our worship: 'do you think I drink the blood of goats, [when] mine are the cattle on a thousand hills?', as the psalmist puts it.[28] But we do.

Late in their relationship with the Indonesian converts of Sumba, the Calvinist missionaries thought it might be a nice cultural gesture to invite the Sumbanese to add their traditional spirit drums to Christian worship. This was because the missionaries didn't believe that the spirit drums called ancestral spirits. But for at least some of those converts, the spirit drums still had power. If they were to say yes, they would not only be playing fast and loose with the power of the drums. They would also

---

27 Leonard Cohen, 'Anthem' from the 1992 album *The Future*.
28 Psalm 50.10, 13.

be saying that Christian worship was itself impervious to that power. By implication, Christian worship was such an internal process that it really didn't need to be a lived event, disruptable by the material power of another faith. The performative efficacy of ritual action in a time and a place with people *doing* things didn't seem to matter to it. Was it still active encounter with the power of God, or was it just making statements *about* God, with the work of worship taking place – or not – in each separate person's heart? Did anything *happen* within the material world in Christian worship?[29]

Durable Fire

Ritual context does not hold God, nor does talking about him invoke his presence. But ritual does give us a range of graspable references for the ineffable being who cannot be held, and formal invocation pleads with a being able – were he so to choose – to offer the dangerous gift of presence. Ritual, then, is a way to connect our physical being in the embodied world of place with that body's creator. The political activist Barbara Ehrenreich wrote a book called *Living with a Wild God: a Non-Believer's Search for the Truth about Everything*. She had personal, cultural and intellectual reasons to walk away from Christianity. But when she had her – unwilled – encounter with the wild God, the image she reached for was the impossible, but impossibly physical, burning bush from Exodus 3:

> At some point on my predawn walk ... the world flamed into life. How else to describe it? There were no visions, no prophetic voices or visits by totemic animals, just this blazing everywhere. Something poured into me and I poured out into it ... It was a furious encounter with a living substance that was coming at me through all things at once, and one

---

29 Webb Keane, *Christian Moderns* (University of California Press, 2007), pp. 223–55.

reason for the terrible wordlessness of the experience is that you cannot observe fire really closely without being part of it. Whether you start as a twig or a gorgeous tapestry, you will be recruited into the flame and made indistinguishable from the rest of the blaze.[30]

Unable, and indeed unwilling, to connect that living experience with the narrow, highly cerebral coercive control of the Christianity she had known, Ehrenreich chose to embrace a belief in a god of place, a *genius loci*, the living divinity of the land. She could only find her way back to the holiness of material stuff – of earth – by leaving the dualist dissociations of modern Christianity behind. At the same time she left behind any reasoned, intellectual approach. Distance was not an option in Ehrenreich's divine experience – either sceptical or assenting. Instead, the boundaries between self and the blazing world were consumed in its fire: 'Something poured into me and I poured out into it ... you cannot observe fire really closely without being part of it.' This is a long way away from statements *about* the divine, or indeed a worshipping culture such as ours that announces God's qualities in a vocative it doubts even as it bespeaks God's presence. We distance ourselves with words rather than submitting to the power of the ritual spaces into which we speak.

In the rare, hard-to-recall times when the blazing weight of God has approached my soul, I have been deeply dismayed as well as awed. The self caught in the presence, whether twig or tapestry, shrinks very small until I no longer see my own extinction as a tragedy, but rather as a moment, a leaf caught in the bonfire of God's essential life. The fierce attention of God upon my soul, the intensity of the approaching blaze, is even more uncomfortable than my abrupt departure from the centre of the stage. I am as much relieved as disappointed (but I am both) when the burning gaze withdraws, leaving the world – yes,

---

30 Barbara Ehrenreich, *Living With a Wild God: a Non-Believer's Search for the Truth about Everything* (Granta, 2001), p. 116.

altered for ever in my understanding of it, but also for the time being its mundane, reassuringly anthropocentric shape again. I recognize Ehrenreich's experience, I even remember it. But I recollect it better in Ralegh's affirmation that 'love is a durable fire'[31] than in the words I hear or say daily at Morning Prayer: 'may the light of your presence, O God, set our hearts on fire with love for you'.[32] Words that seem strangely hedged and observational, nothing much stronger than a lukewarm wish, rather as you say to an acquaintance, 'Let's meet up sometime' without really meaning to follow it up.

'You that sought for magic in your youth'[33]

The performatives of ritual have withdrawn from our public culture and public places, in Christianity as in secularized culture. They have been replaced by assertions of feeling that claim the improbable authority of sincerity (though often the words used will neither express nor reliably invoke the feeling they claim to convey). But those same performatives have burgeoned in our imaginative lives, in the realm of the unbodied and securely fictive. The modern fantasy genre, set off more or less by accident by the Catholic J. R. R. Tolkien, features words that make things happen, objects infused with power that change people's natures, numinous rituals in numinous places, sacred journeys, and more sublime and semi-sentient landscape than you can shake a magic staff at.

---

31 '[L]ove is a durable fire, In the mind ever burning; Never sick, never old, never dead; From itself never turning'. Sir Walter Ralegh, 'As you came from the holy land/Of Walsingham', in *Sir Walter Ralegh: Selected Writings*, ed. Gerald Hammond (Carcanet Press, 1984), p. 36.

32 *Common Worship: Daily Prayer* (Church House Publishing, 2005), p. 115.

33 Lord Dunsany, *The King of Elfland's Daughter* (1924), quoted in Alan Jacobs, 'Fantasy and the Buffered Self', *New Atlantis* (Winter, 2014), https://www.thenewatlantis.com/publications/fantasy-and-the-buffered-self (accessed 14.2.2023).

In a 2014 article called 'Fantasy and the Buffered Self', the literary critic Alan Jacobs argues that fantasy is the genre that allows the modern person to be open to enchantment while still feeling safe. He is drawing here on the philosopher Charles Taylor's definition of the pre-modern self as 'porous' – open to 'forces' (whether these were demons, fairies, angels, *genius loci*, or the presence of God) that could shape human lives from the outside. Taylor distinguishes this state of being from the modern 'buffered self', which has (as he puts it) a 'much firmer boundary between self and other'. The buffered self is protected (or at any rate feels itself protected) from the many dangers of being open to forces beyond its control; but in viewing the universe mechanically, and keeping its sensibility separate from the phenomena it observes, it is lonely. Paraphrasing the thought of Ralph Waldo Emerson, Jacobs writes:

> the problem is that we exist but the world around us does not, or does not in the same way we do. It is either dead or a fictional projection of our perceptions. But a disenchanted world then spreads its disenchantment to us.[34]

It is this separation between self and world that was so ferociously dissolved in Ehrenreich's 'burning bush' encounter. It will, perhaps, come as no surprise to learn that her mental and emotional breakdown was not long after – though quite ambiguously associated with – Ehrenreich's strikingly non-buffered experience.

No one wants to invite breakdown. So it is, writes Jacobs, that modernity finds its enchantment in safely fictional form, in

> the rise to cultural prominence, in late modernity, of the artistic genre of *fantasy*. Fantasy – in books, films, television shows, and indeed in all imaginable media – is an instrument by which the late modern self strives to avail itself of the unpredictable excitements of the porous self while retaining its

---

34 Quoted in Jacobs, 'Fantasy and the Buffered Self'.

protective buffers. Fantasy, in most of its recent forms, may best be understood as a technologically enabled, and there-fore *safe*, simulacrum of the pre-modern porous self.[35]

Jacobs' article goes on to observe that although fantasy's mod-ern consumers may rely on the full fictive separation of the genre, a number of its most influential originators (he cites the notably Christian Tolkien and C. S. Lewis) didn't see it that way: 'Tolkien may not have believed in Sauron, but he surely believed that there are in human history people who sell them-selves to the Enemy and find themselves as a result ... first empowered and then destroyed.' Nor (according to Tolkien himself) was he offering this perception as allegory, or even as metaphor. 'I cordially dislike allegory in all its manifestations' he wrote, 'and always have done so since I grew old and wary enough to detect its presence. I much prefer history – true or feigned – with its varied applicability to the thought and experi-ence of readers.'[36] In other words, Tolkien writes as he does because the world indeed works this way.

Yet, as Jacobs also hints, the attraction of the genre for its modern consumers is not straightforwardly or even mainly its fictiveness. The gift of fantasy, whether for children or adults, is its promise that reality is more integrated and responsive between self and world than we can allow ourselves to think in our directly mundane experience. It's a *fuller* place to inhabit than the dead world of external observation. And, in it, words are more than reflections: they bespeak a living power. This is the longed-for but also deeply feared place of *poesis*, or *making*, where, as Samuel Taylor Coleridge once put it in a letter:

> are not words etc parts and germinations of the plant? And what is the Law of the Growth? In something of this order I would endeavour to destroy the old antithesis of *Words and*

---

35 Jacobs, 'Fantasy and the Buffered Self'.

36 J. R. R. Tolkien, 'Foreword', in *The Fellowship of the Ring*, vol. 1 of *The Lord of the Rings* (HarperCollins, 2nd edn, 1999), p. xviii.

Things, elevating, as it were, words into Things, and living Things too.[37]

For, even as they see 'knowledge' as the lonely intelligence analysing passive externals, modern human beings cannot help but desire the kind of knowing that – however dangerously – seeks to know them back. That threadbare word 'interactive' reaches, however impotently, towards a mutual responsiveness between self and world that is our lost birthright.

Growing into reading in the late 1960s, I took it as entirely natural that the books I read opened up an enchanted world. Because *The Hobbit* was almost the first book I read by myself, at I suppose about five, *The Lord of the Rings* rapidly followed; and at six, or even seven, the divide between fictive enchantment and the real world is narrow indeed. Who knows what of that monumental read I actually followed – I can't tell at this distance, though I have a clear memory of chanting Galadriel's lament to myself, *by heart, in Elvish*, in the infants' playground – but for a while I certainly believed I was reading history, not story, and that I was living in an overrun and modernized future Shire. I realized, of course, that Tolkien was offering the story as story – I didn't mistake it for documentary – but decided I was being given a necessarily hidden truth. And the evidence was there, I thought. Bilbo lived in Hobbiton, and down the road was Bywater – obvious and transparent disguises for Woking (where I lived) and Byfleet, home to my grandparents and cousins. It perhaps helped that my grandparents were clear Edwardians in the way the hobbits were; their house was stark and new (probably built by some version of Ted Sandyman) but beyond the front door were the heavy sideboards, the umbrella stand, the deal chests, waistcoats, collar buttons and (out the back) neat vegetable plots of the old world.

---

37 Quoted in Stephen Prickett, *Words and the Word* (Cambridge University Press, 1986), and part of a highly relevant discussion of Prickett's book by Adam Roberts in relation to Coleridge. See https://samueltaylorbloggeridge.blogspot.com/2016/07/pricketts-words-and-word-1986-and.html (accessed 14.2.2023).

I read Tolkien's explanation in his 1960 essay 'Concerning Hobbits' as to why hobbits were so hard to encounter since Men became dominant, and it seemed pure sense to me. Around me Woking Council tore down the small Edwardian town I first knew, so I understood very well what Sam Gamgee saw in Galadriel's mirror. I was not at all interested in the stripped-down, modernist, concrete present of the 1970s; and neat Surrey, where the woods were all narrow borders to roads or railways and the green spaces highly managed, gave only faltering promises of wildness. I looked for the signs and remnants of ancient things – the Roman camp at Bisley, the barren bits of gorse and moor, the strange tower on Leith Hill – and concluded that the enchanted world was in deep retreat, but not gone. It was hiding within its own history.

A remarkable proportion of the books I (and so my contemporaries) read looked backwards. Alan Garner's *Weirdstone of Brisingamen* and *The Moon of Gomrath*, Lucy Boston's *Green Knowe* books, Philippa Pearce's *Tom's Midnight Garden*, Penelope Farmer's *Charlotte Sometimes*, Kipling's *Puck of Pook's Hill* and *Rewards and Fairies*, John Masefield's *The Midnight Folk* and *Box of Delights*, Susan Cooper's Arthurian *Over Sea, Under Stone* that began *The Dark is Rising* sequence, Joan G. Robinson's heartbreaking *When Marnie Was There*.[38] All were books of place, landscapes remembering former inhabitants,

---

38 Alan Garner, *The Weirdstone of Brisingamen* (William Collins & Sons, 1960); Alan Garner, *The Moon of Gomrath* (William Collins & Sons, 1963); Lucy Boston, *The Children of Green Knowe* (Faber and Faber, 1954); the rest of the Green Knowe series of six books appeared from Faber between 1954 and 1976; Philippa Pearce, *Tom's Midnight Garden* (Oxford University Press, 1958); Penelope Farmer, *Charlotte Sometimes* (Chatto & Windus, 1969); Rudyard Kipling, *Puck of Pook's Hill* (Macmillan & Co, 1906); Rudyard Kipling, *Rewards and Fairies* (Macmillan & Co, 1910); John Masefield, *The Midnight Folk* (Heinemann, 1927); John Masefield, *The Box of Delights* (Heinemann, 1935); Susan Cooper, *Over Sea, Under Stone* (London: Jonathan Cape, 1965); Joan G. Robinson, *When Marnie Was There* (William Collins & Sons, 1967).

vanished or hidden ways: Macclesfield and Alderley Edge, the Fens, Sussex, Cornwall, the north Norfolk coast.

Among them Alan Garner's *Elidor*, where the cruel, chivalrous otherworld breaks through into 1960s slum-clearance Manchester, puzzled and troubled me.[39] I knew the Manchester landscape from visits to my grandma in Bury before the M6 was finished, and had longed for the power to rebuild the lines of derelict, half-destroyed terraces (my grandma lived in such a terrace, with a CONDEMNED sign on the adjoining empty house) and make them into homes again. For once, the fantasy land of Elidor seemed less real than the pathos of the destroyed neighbourhoods, the jutting mantelpieces exposed to the air, the bright peeling wallpapers of lost bedrooms and sitting-rooms. Ruins and fragments are that book's real power. Years later, I read Robert Roberts on his childhood in Salford before the First World War, and recognized the immediate precursor to my grandma's world. In his autobiography, *A Ragged Schooling*, Roberts remembers sitting up on the hills as an adult, watching the demolition of the grim terraces of his childhood going on down below and thinking, yes, of course they should go, but there goes my life too.[40]

For my generation of children, the First World War (more, I think, than the Second), and the lost world it broke, haunted the landscapes and stories we consumed. Chief among them was the *Lord of the Rings* itself, so that the Great War, disguised within an artificially pre-industrial landscape, still permeates the whole fantasy genre; but of the other books I have cited a remarkable number have Edwardian ghosts for their hauntings.[41]

---

39 Alan Garner, *Elidor* (William Collins & Sons, 1965).

40 Robert Roberts, *The Classic Slum* (Manchester University Press, 1971); Robert Roberts, *A Ragged Schooling* (Manchester University Press, 1976).

41 The psychedelic music of the hippy Seventies in its English form (the American one is more interested in Vietnam) shows a parallel Edwardian/Great War haunting, whether prominently in the Beatles, *Sergeant Pepper and his Lonely Hearts Club Band* (1967), or more mutedly in the Kinks, 'The Village Green Preservation Society' (1969);

As well as those books explicitly rooted in the geography of an England reluctant to say farewell to its rewards and fairies, there were and are those set in imagined places, uncoincidentally pre-industrial otherwheres where the rules of reality are responsively different. The early fantasy practitioners thought very seriously about the earth-shaking qualities of words that could alter the nature of things. In Ursula Le Guin's *Earthsea* series, the magic required to change a loaf of bread into something else was infinitely more costly to its worker than the spectacular magic of illusion; names were powerful magic, to be used sparingly; and the wielding or invoking of the world's powers would be dangerous to the immature, the arrogant and the thoughtless.[42] That caution about the nature of enchantment pervades the best of adult fantasy, as in the dangers of the world of Susanna Clarke's *Jonathan Strange and Mr Norrell*.[43] *Jonathan Strange* itself draws on a strand of modern fiction that played with Faerie, whether Sylvia Townsend Warner's *Kingdoms of Elfin* (among others) or Hope Mirrlees' *Lud-in-the-Mist*.[44]

Only in retrospect has it struck me how very strange it was that the vast majority of 1970s (and later) children's books dealt so constantly and intensively with the magic conspicuously absent from ordinary life. If anything, this has intensified over the decades, resulting in the passionate double life of many children (including as, and after, they became adults) in the Harry Potter world where words (in Latin, naturally, as all *hoc est corpus* must be) really do make stuff happen (*lumos, accio*),

---

or Stackridge, *The Man in the Bowler Hat* (1973), or Robyn Hitchcock. But that's another story, for which I am indebted to the insights and research of Sam Inglis.

42 Ursula le Guin's original Earthsea trilogy: *The Wizard of Earthsea* (Parnassus Press, 1968), *The Tombs of Atuan* (Atheneum Books, 1971), *The Farthest Shore* (Atheneum Books, 1972) were followed by further sequels in 1990 and 2001.

43 Susanna Clarke, *Jonathan Strange and Mr Norrell* (Bloomsbury, 2004).

44 Sylvia Townsend Warner, *Kingdoms of Elfin* (Viking Books, 1977); Hope Mirrlees, *Lud-in-the-Mist* (William Collins & Sons, 1926).

and the real platform at King's Cross Station provides a place for pilgrims to film themselves passing over into the otherworld of magical efficacy on Platform 9¾.[45]

Unreal Engines

The nominalist tropes of fantasy are both a commonplace and a gift for the internet, where code really does (in a sense) make things happen, and children can find out their Patronus on a website.[46] In the quest-and-contest online fantasy, *Fairy Tail*, the magic category 'Solid Script' confers the power to bring about a change in the world through writing the word for that change.[47] *Fiat lux*, at your fingertips. In a two-dimensional world, the third dimension is itself fantasy. In other formulaic spinoffs of the online world, for example the videogames of magical quests, the avatar runs with the ease and strength of thought, simulating just enough friction with the world of the game to keep the idea of embodiment vaguely plausible. What she runs through, though, is still a numinous landscape of temples and statues, sacred rocks and physical puzzles. These worlds are frequently ruined, often falling as she runs; like Tolkien's middle earth, they are full of remnants and signs.

If you were, for example, to visit the website of Unreal Engine, proud makers of game worlds, you might find a demo showing what Unreal Engine 5.0 can do; and therefore pick a typical landscape, which like many such landscapes owes a good deal to Indiana Jones on his way to pick up the Ark of the Covenant.[48] The demo's intention is to show the finesse with which

---

45 https://harrypottershop.co.uk/pages/platform934 (accessed 14.2.2023).

46 https://www.wizardingworld.com/news/discover-your-patronus-on-pottermore (accessed 14.2.2023).

47 https://fairytail.fandom.com/wiki/Solid_Script (accessed 14.2.2023).

48 https://www.unrealengine.com/en-US (accessed 14.2.2023). See also www.youtube.com/watch?v=qC5KtatMcUw, from 1 min 22 secs (accessed 14.2.2023).

their technology can create any world a games designer cares to specify. They are particularly proud of the way they make the light fall, and the physically plausible interaction between the avatar's body and the world's surfaces, with properly gripping hands and convincing squeezes through narrow places. Though the avatar continues to have a video body, impervious to hurt or danger, she climbs like she means it – and she flies like she just doesn't care.

The technicians of virtual reality continue to work out how to make it feel as if the player is *inside* such a world in their real, actual body; they can get the perspective but not the touch, and it's a problem not to be able to see your feet. They want it 'realler', but with all the whizz of unreality added in and no real-world consequences. In comparison, the earthbound, vulnerable ritual of eucharist seems slow indeed.

Theatre once reflected back to audiences, often powerfully and uncomfortably, the things they held most sacred. We have seen something of how unsettling that was in the first generations after the Reformation. As soon as theatre became securely fictive, its sacred force muted by secular indifference and distance, its range of influence became confined to comment, or even to a consumer delicacy. The other forms of imagined worlds we visit now have the same problem. In most of them, the holy fragments still scattered around the culture are treated like props (why is there a character in *The Matrix* called Trinity? Why is Keanu Reeves wearing a *soutane*?), apparently in the hope that the chance-come grail will fizzle belatedly to life and glow in the watcher's hands. It seems to me urgent that the world of eucharist should not follow suit and turn into pure entertainment. Not least because, as entertainment, it can't, even in its supposedly fizziest form, compete with flying off a mountain into the setting sun.

The Synecdochic Lever

The theoretician of place, space and architecture, Robert Harbison, says this of maps:

> From cities of bricks to cities in books to cities on maps is a path of increasing conceptualization. A map seems the type of the conceptual object, yet the interesting thing is the grotesquely token foot it keeps in the world of the physical, having the unreality without the far-fetched appropriateness of the edibles in communion, being a picture to the extent that the sacrament is a meal.[49]

Flat maps give us the shape and orientation of something they can't replicate in all dimensions: they are a very precise, very detailed version of the rhetorical figure *synecdoche*, where the part stands for the whole. *Synecdoche*, rather than simile, might also be the figure that describes the physicality of eucharist, where the elements are small but, like Donne's dying body, contain and transform the world. As we receive, our mortal bodies like flat maps tracing the contours of our being, we take into ourselves that transformation and find ourselves remade in the new dimension. This is not fantasy. It is a performative, invoking the power of God.

Imagine, then, the eucharist as an act of sacred theatre, its symbols working like levers to open a door – small in themselves, but fulcrums for a movement that changes the whole meaning of the space. As with all good theatre, the irreducible elements are simple: space, bodies, words: a table laid with the basic food and drink of life. You can, and might, choose to have more than this, to use the whole aesthetic panoply; or you might be starkly plain.

While all theatre requires an audience, sacred theatre requires those who come to be both auditors and participants, both

49 Robert Harbison, *Eccentric Spaces* (MIT Press, 1977), p. 124, quoted in Jonathan Z. Smith, *To Take Place* (University of Chicago Press, 1992), p. 74.

acted-upon and actors. Whatever their reasons for entering the sacred space (however that sacred space is defined), they do not expect to leave unchanged. This is not passive viewing. It is a process that they will undergo.

Those who provide the movements in the drama play out their function. That function is more than a *persona*, but also more significant than the person's individual character. Individual character may be part of what they use to exercise their function well, but character is subsumed into the demands of function. And because of this, personal character flaw cannot undermine the drama. Set apart to play out the breaks and cracks in human nature and human love in the eyes of God, the actors know that they, being part of those breaks and cracks, are appropriate vehicles for the drama of mending and restoration. They were chosen, not because they were strong, but simply because they *were* chosen. They are representative. They are obedient to that representative calling, whether of priest or musician, reader or intercessor, server or preacher.

Eucharist, not *Eucatastrophe*

The grounds of the drama are tragic. Its losses are real and terrible. If that is not visible, then the drama is not real either. Eucharist is not *eucatastrophe*, where the tragic plot is reversed into comic fulfilment at the very last minute.[50] The eucharist shows something that is beyond the very last minute. It is

---

50 The critic Adam Roberts expresses scepticism on *eucatastrophe* specifically in relation to Tolkien's plot (the word itself is Tolkien's, coined in *On Fairy Stories*), which Roberts thinks impels readers to believe that last-minute rescues from apparently hopeless circumstances are, as it were, baked into the meaning of the world, and therefore release humanity from attempting to rescue situations (climate change, for example) before they become hopeless. But neither the Passion nor, therefore, the promise of eucharist are eucatastrophic. They are tragic. They are also beyond tragic. See https://medium.com/adams-notebook/two-thoughts-on-eucatastrophe-e2fc62f97a3c (accessed 14.2.2023).

what happens on the other side of *too late*. It does not cancel mortality, but it sanctifies it. Its matter for wonder is that anything *but* loss could be brought out of such sorrow, such wrong. But as we look upon it, we also understand that we witness a miracle of reversal. We come here to weep, but we realize that our weeping is for a love made tangible, present in touch, in taste, in the mortal body itself. That we will not *only* die, and we will not *only* fail. We are also here to be made alive, to be freed from every debt. Because we fell, helpless to save ourselves, we are lifted up again.

'Therefore, that he may raise, the Lord throws down.'[51]

---

51 John Donne, 'Hymn to God, My God, in My Sickness'.

4

The Eucharist in Time

Advent Prose

Jessica said, 'Oh, I remember ...' but didn't go on. She was remembering other Advents, and hedges snowy as sheep from her window, and the Star ready to be pasted up on the sky again.

Roger pulled over, and they watched the scuffed and dun military going in to evensong. The wind smelled of fresh snow.

'We ought to be home,' she said, after a bit, 'it's late.'

'We could just pop in here for a minute.'

Well, that surprised her, but def, after weeks of his snide comments? His unbeliever's annoyance with the others in Psi Section he thought were out to drive him dotty as they were, and his Scroogery growing as shopping days to Xmas dwindle – 'You're not supposed to be the sort', she told him. But she did want to go in, nostalgia was heavy in tonight's snow-sky, her own voice ready to betray her and run to join the waits whose carols we are so apt to hear now in the distances, these days of Advent dropping one by one, voices piping across frozen downs where the sown mines crowd thick as plums in a pudding ... often above sounds of melting snow, winds that must blow not through Christmas air but through substance of time would bring her those child-voices, singing for sixpences, and if her heart wasn't quite ready to take on quite all the stresses of her mortality and theirs, at least there was the fear that she was beginning to lose them – that one winter she would go running to look, out to the gate to find them, run as far as the trees but in vain, their voices fading ...

They walked through the tracks of all the others in the snow, she gravely on his arm, wind blowing her hair to snarls, heels slipping once on ice. 'To hear the music', he explained.[1]

Thomas Pynchon's layered, copious and encyclopaedic novel, *Gravity's Rainbow*, from which this extract is taken, was published in 1973 and set towards the end of the Second World War. War – ordered, large-scale human violence in a responsively violent world – is its occasion and its matter, the body's desires its motor. This passage, from the novel's opening section 'Beyond the Zero', occurs in Kent in the last week of Advent (a period that also opens the Church year), looking towards Christmas 1944.

What you read here is only the beginning of an extended, various and technically astonishing set-piece meditation (8 pages in the Picador edition) set within the timeframe of the evensong the couple attends. The liturgy itself is compressed and represented by a couple of short quotations from the macaronic medieval carol *In Dulci Jubilo*, one near the meditation's beginning and one towards its end. The choir sings in Latin and German ('the *German*? In an English church?' runs the internal commentary that swiftly escapes Jessica's seeing or thought):

In dulci jubilo
Nun singet und seid froh!
Unsers Herzen Wonne
Leit in presipio,
Leuchtet vor die Sonne
Matris in gremio.
Alpha es et O.[2]

---

1 Thomas Pynchon, *Gravity's Rainbow* (Picador, 1975), pp. 127–8. First published in Great Britain by Jonathan Cape, 1973. All quotations that follow are from this edition and fall between pp. 127–36.

2 Translation: In sweet rejoicing, sing now and be glad! Our hearts' bliss lies in the manger; And he shines like the sun in his mother's lap. You are the beginning [the Alpha] and the end [the Omega].

We watch the choir sing this first verse while the free-running narrative voice bounces our seeing across the 'intricate needs of the Anglo-American empire' and the time-layered world of the sounds we readers cannot hear, making us wheel towards and then away from the singers (especially a tall Jamaican counter-tenor) making music in 'this cold fieldmouse church', channelling through their modern bodies sound-structures made centuries ago by 'Thomas Tallis, Henry Purcell ... the fifteenth-century macronic [sic] attributed to Heinrich Suso.'

'Listen', the narrator says to us, 'this is the War's evensong, the War's canonical hour, and the night is real.' And next we are away into that real night, our regard up high and looking down, like the perspective at the very beginning of Powell and Pressburger's film *A Matter of Life and Death*, but infinitely precise, flying above and beyond the Wrens who 'work late', following what happens to the mass of squeezed toothpaste tubes as they wait to be made into munitions, the lingering menthol of the bubbles spat into plugholes by 'thousands of children' and absorbed into sewers and then the sea, through the sensibility of a 'long time schiz, you know, who believes he *is* World War II' and towards that Bethlehem stable... Then back away from that vision towards Italian prisoners of war managing the mail sacks full of Christmas cards, dreaming the 'nearly postwar luxury of buying an electric train set for the kid ... the plaster baby, the oxen frosted with gold leaf and the human-eyed sheep are turning real again, paint quickens to flesh ... he is the New Baby'. Back away again, across the sensibilities of the old, the grandparents, towards time and its violences, 'the old faces turn to the clock faces, thinking *plot*, and the numbers go whirling towards the Nativity, a violence, a nova of heart that will turn us all, change us forever to the very forgotten roots of who we are.' And back away again again across the landscape, watching travellers who might be pilgrims unknowing or knowing, landing briefly with the NAAFI girls 'named Eileen, carefully sorting into refrigerated compartments the rubbery maroon organs with their yellow garnishes of fat – oh Linda come here feel this one, put your finger down in the ventricle here, isn't it swoony, it's still going'. And back away again again again melding the centuries so that the Bethlehem census merges with the endless record-keeping of twentieth century total war – 'and the local hookers are keeping the foreskinned invaders happy, charging whatever the traffic will bear, just like the innkeepers who're naturally delighted with this registration thing, and up in the capital they're wondering should they, maybe, give everybody a *number*, yeah, something to help SPQR record-keeping' ...

And then pause: a dream, unfulfilled, of arriving.

But on the way home tonight, you wish you'd picked him up, held him a bit. Just held him, very close to your heart, his cheek by the hollow of your shoulder, full of sleep. As if it were you who could, somehow, save him. For the moment not caring who you're supposed to be registered as. For the moment anyway, no longer who the Caesars say you are.

> O Jesu parvule
> Nach dir is mir so weh ...[3]

Heartache is the understated pulse ('for the moment') of this long ambitious view, an extended *bravura* that may only come to meet the love that powers it in picturing an instant out of reach, whether in a vanishing past or a present that never came to be. The span of centuries and places, of the multifarious material *stuff*, the politics of desire and greed, the violence of control and of detonation: all come across the reader's inner world in the moment it takes to sing ten phrases of music in imagined wartime Kent – about 40 seconds in 'real time'. Slipping in and out of sight lies the promised incarnation, maybe the 'infant prince', wise maker of the universe, or else a tiny mortal helpless in the grip of mundane cruelties. 'Is the baby smiling, or is it just gas? Which do you want it to be?'

---

3 Translation: O little Jesus, my heart aches for you.

Pynchon's imaginative reach is as big as he can make it. That's big – but the limits of being constrain even him. And these constraints he both manages and disguises by gesturing outside what can be said as often as (if not oftener than) he can get away with it. He sidesteps time through his copiousness, the encyclopaedic reach of his novelist's eye, much as a long epic poem might seek to reify the world it makes through its very length and detail. It's both successful and extremely exhausting – too much for this particular reader, honestly, too continual a violence, but an extraordinary and paradoxical defiance of limit, all the same. Just here, eternity is the ghost in this huge machine; and it looks like a newborn, like the body of Jesus promised as an ambiguous joy to our joy-destroying world. In Thomas Pynchon's Advent prose, loss and gift are wrapped up so tight together that they cannot be separated.

There and not-there

Pynchon writes of the body of Jesus – imagined here, on the threshold of the Incarnation, as a child's body – as something both there and not-there. The war's babies and children come in and out of his view; the particular experience of holding the child Jesus is imagined as something that never quite happened, or perhaps as an event so long ago, so ambiguously historical, that it could only be invoked in a vision of loss. Time circles around the possibility of the baby, symptom of a modern consciousness that cannot assent to the object of yearning but cannot quite discard it either. This is a very modern devotional, closer to lament than joy, able neither to trust nor to let it go.

'The War's canonical hour' is an evensong, not a eucharist; but we have met this devotional mode before. For in our modern, historically fractured eucharists, the body of Jesus, God's physicality in the world of things, is also both there and not-there. Is bread always and only bread? As Luther observes – in a rather Pynchonesque moment – we can neither 'chew nor slurp' God as we would chew or slurp the food of the mundane world, yet (as Luther also says) what makes the ritual food of bread and wine into God is invoked through language spoken by an absent mouth, in Christ's absent body, in another time.[4] Jesus makes bread into himself here and now by an utterance spoken long ago across a temporal gulf, dying away into the silence of a finished sentence, running the interference of intervening history, fragmented in remembrance, attenuated, altered, narrated, reshaped, translated, questioned, rejected, reanimated, reiterated, performed, re-formed. Loss and absence have a speaking power in the modern eucharist, just as they do for Pynchon, who can neither believe nor leave belief alone. Bread both is, and is not, always and only bread. We can neither agree about, nor dispense with, Christ's presence.

This temporal aspect is the ground of the eucharist's being, as well as its main problem. Because the communion is a re-membering of Jesus's body, when we ask whether and how Christ is present we are in effect asking how he can be present in *this* particular instant of time – how the past from which the words of institution come, how the historic moment of Christ's life on earth, can be aligned with the present we physically inhabit. And, as in Pynchon's extended *bravura*, time circles around the possibility of the absent presence of that body. 'What happened enters into the house of what is always happening, and sits with it together, and eats at its table', writes Patricia Lockwood.

Time, memory and the eucharist

This chapter is about the eucharist in time. One of the points on which all understandings of the eucharist are agreed is that it is an act of *remembering*, an obedient response to Jesus's invitation: 'Do this in remembrance of me'. So I write here about the relationship we experience between memory and time (memory

---

4 Luther, 'Vom Abendmahl Christi' (1528) quoted Phyllis Mack, *Visionary Women* (University of California Press, 1992), p. 21.

being the way that we apprehend time's passing), looking at how the work of memory bears upon the ritual of eucharist, where *what was* comes to abide with *what is* and reaches towards *what will be*.

All the patterning and ordering of human life, all its meaning-making, is dependent upon acts of memory. So I am also thinking about these eucharistic understandings of memory and time as they arise in the notional Now of modernity, a Now where we have particular cultural conditions that exert pressure upon the relationships we assume between memory and time passing. I look particularly at the intersection of cultural and personal memory, both as it works itself out in the devotional experience of eucharistic ritual and as it plays out in modern human experience.

Poesis

Bringing the past to bear upon the present is not unique to the eucharist. And the transformation of any present moment by the memory of past acts will shape expectations of an invisible future. All acts of memory have this shape – absolutely everything human beings do to join the past to the present to the future. We make the absent (the past; the future) present through a linguistic *poesis* or making: 'the bringing of something into being'. And, though modernity is much more comfortable with the idea of language as something that reflects (with more or less accuracy) what already really exists without the distortions of speech, it's also the case that linguistic patternings and structures deliberately play with time in order to shape our sense of what the vanishing point of present-ness may even contain. We make meaning with the raw material of time.

Copiousness is only one of the forms people choose to side-step linear time. It is the one Pynchon chose, but it's not the most common. The designation of a small but mobile time-unit – a poem, a musical phrase, a patterned verbal utterance – as 'the present' is another, commoner way to order and indeed alter the experience of time. So it is that the poet-musician Don Paterson characterizes sonnet form as iterating present-ness – 'approximately thirteen[5] instances of the present moment'[6] even though the time it takes to read (even silently) a single pentameter line has duration in which linear time really falls into the past. He describes the sonnet as a form with its 'tail in its mouth', coming back to its beginning as it closes, but with the experience of the lines between altering the reader's apprehension of that beginning. In this way the sonnet form is 'symbolic of both transformation and unity: we've returned to precisely the same point as we started, but have ascended in pitch or moved forward in time, so in the song's singing, in the idea's thinking, something is transformed, yet stays the same'.[7]

The work of memory is exactly this kind of work, on every span of the human scale. It binds what has passed to what is being experienced, tying them together into an apprehensible unit that can be called 'present' because its pattern repeats enough to be recognized, or 'known again': days, years, habits, seasons, and all their smaller patterns. This is a continual work of making to which we are so accustomed that we do not see it as making at all. We elide it, instead, with the continually elusive experience of being in time, and so we do not notice how actively we shape our relationship with time in making meaning.

Full, perfect and sufficient[8]

Yet when Jesus says to his companions 'Do this in remembrance of me' – tying the present moment of the broken bread,

---

5 Paterson offers a number of speculative reasons about why thirteen lines might be 'righter' than fourteen as a perfect poetic unit, but they are not strictly relevant here.

6 Don Paterson, 'Introduction', *101 Sonnets* (Faber & Faber, 1999), pp. xxv–xxvi.

7 Paterson, 'Introduction', pp. xix–xx.

8 Christ's 'full, perfect and sufficient sacrifice, oblation and satisfac-

the poured wine, to the living body that will in the unseen future of tomorrow be broken and spilled, extinguished and then restored, brought round into being again once and for all like a sonnet's cadence – when he speaks and acts his eucharistic pattern, Jesus remakes the meaning of every created thing. And this he does through an everyday, ephemeral utterance, a domestic service, falling into the nothing of pastness like every unrecorded meal, every loving word ever spoken that fell into silence. There was no stenographer in the corner as Jesus tied yesterday to today and for ever; but those to whom he spoke did as he asked. They remembered. The act subsists still, tying the fleeting now to a then that changed what 'now' could be. It was ordinary, and it was unique: full, perfect and sufficient.

Then we preserved it in a ritual, an iterating picture of presentness, and called it (among other things) *eucharist*, 'thanksgiving'.

---

tion for the sins of the whole world', a 'one oblation of himself once offered', is declared by the priest just before the Words of Institution in the *Book of Common Prayer* (in all versions). See *Book of Common Prayer*, ed. Cummings (2013), p. 402. It is a moment of doctrinal specificity, supporting Article XXXI of the 39 Articles, which states that the 'Offering of Christ once made is that perfect redemption, propitiation, and satisfaction, for all the sins of the whole world, both original and actual; and there is none other satisfaction for sin, but that alone. Wherefore the sacrifices of Masses, in the which it was commonly said, that the Priest did offer Christ for the quick and the dead, to have remission of pain or guilt, were blasphemous fables, and dangerous deceits.' It is therefore part of an unresolved argument between reformed and catholic about the intentions and kind(s) of efficacy ascribed to the rite's iteration, given the unique nature of Christ's original act of redemption. I touch on the difficulties on all sides of this argument, but note that Protestant and Catholic alike accept the principle of ceremonial reiteration, while ascribing to its practice different kinds of value. See https://www.churchofengland.org/prayer-and-worship/worship-texts-and-resources/book-common-prayer/articles-religion#XXXI (accessed 14.2.2023).

'Let your Communion Be at Least in Listening'[9]

When people look for ways to connect fleetingness with for ever, their most common recourse is repetition. The circular medium of a repeated action or sound imposes an image of restoration upon the 'ever rolling stream' of linear time. Or, as Adam Seligman puts it in his book *Ritual and its Consequences*, repetition 'can mitigate the effects of time, denying the ontological character of the new in favour of what is beyond time'.[10] For this reason rituals of worship, including Christian ones, employ a lot of repetition. The techniques of repetition are used across liturgical structure, from the macro- to the micro-scale, nesting within one another like puzzle-boxes. So ritual patterning reiterates across years and times and seasons; actions and words repeat through each single liturgical event. And, within the event, sacred repetition is vital to that highly evocative medium of pattern, rhythm and sound – music.

For music – as well as in reality being a powerful player within ritual – also works effectively as a concentrated metaphor for the sacred efficacy of repetition. Pynchon's set-piece, 'canonical office' though he calls it, actually solely employs music to indicate the trans-temporal power of the liturgy that his protagonists attend. Music is both the excuse for them entering ('"To hear the music", he explained') and the matter of Roger and Jessica's experience, the carrier for what happens to them. 'Listen to this mock-angel singing', writes Pynchon, 'let your communion be at least in listening, even if they are not spokesmen for your exact hopes, your exact, darkest terror, listen.' In the nine quoted lines (in singing, ten) of one medieval Christmas carol Pynchon deploys musical phrase as an enclosed, repeatable eternity-capsule, folding transcendence up as small as the instructions within a seed, 'heven and erth

---

9 Thomas Pynchon, *Gravity's Rainbow* (Picador, 1975), p. 138.
10 Adam Seligman and Robert P. Weller, *Ritual and its Consequences* (Oxford University Press, 2008), p. 121.

THE EUCHARIST IN TIME

in litel space'[11]– to effect a trans-temporal vision of an elusive felicity:

There must have been evensong here long before the news of Christ. Surely for as long as there have been nights bad as this one – something to raise the possibility of another night that could actually, with love and cockcrows, light the path home, banish the Adversary, destroy the boundaries between our lands, our bodies, our stories, all false, about who we are: for the one night, leaving only the clear way home and the memory of the infant you saw, almost too frail ...[12]

'Materialized Memory'[13]

Pynchon gets his atheist Roger over the sacred threshold with music because music's trans-temporal power spreads well beyond the sacred realm. It always has, of course – sacred and profane have always cross-fertilized, music has always been both necessary and disruptive to sacred ritual – but in our time of late modernity, music challenges the dominance of time with a significant difference. It is a general truth that our wider cultural 'communion ... [is] at least in listening'. Recorded music is the main mode by which we hear, the emotional background to living: it is everywhere. A little child will be much more likely to hear recorded music than living song. We have an extraordinarily efficient means to 'deny the ontological character of the new', and we employ it constantly. We don't call it sacred, but it meets Seligman's definition of ritual very neatly.

---

11 'heven and erth in litel space' describes Jesus in the womb of Mary within the fifteenth-century carol 'Ther is no rose'. Trin. Coll. Camb. MS O.3.58.

12 Pynchon, p. 135.

13 The phrase is Mark Fisher's, describing recorded popular music. 'Why Hauntology?', in 'The Slow Cancellation of the Future', *Ghosts of My Life: Writings on Depression, Hauntology and Lost Futures* (Zero Books, 2014).

The Marxist writer Mark Fisher calls these precise electronic iterations of past sound 'materialized memory'. He is talking about something very different from Pynchon's evocation of a unique musical performance, sung by particular bodies, particular voices, unrecorded, at one particular time in their lives and the history of the world, and then gone. Fisher is talking about sounds that do not go away and cannot change their qualities. These are not a set of performances of the same piece. Often they are not even one performance – what we hear cannot be traced back to a complete, single and historical hearing experience caught in time and then replicated.[14] Rather, it was constructed in bits and put together technologically, adjusted for listening so that its finished technological rendition had its artists hearing it for the first time as a complete artefact.

It is not at all weird to us that we live constantly with the precise electronic repetition of a vanished event – but it is unique. It's never happened before in the history of the world. And these chunks of memory are not really about the memory of the performance. It may never have happened as a performance in any case; and the laborious conditions of its piecemeal construction are hidden from its hearers. These artefacts are designed to be triggers for the memory of those who consume them. All day, every day, memory can be brought vividly into present feeling by the exact replication of songs heard at another stage of life: in first love, first loss, in bitterness or bereavement or trouble.

Frequently now those songs are sung by the dead, and even those singers who still live will be more present to us in their vanished, young, carefree forms than in the ageing selves and

---

14 The extraordinary fascination of the Peter Jackson edit of the Beatles' 1969 recording session (*The Beatles: Get Back*, 2021) is discovering just how many different renditions there could be of the same piece, when each one of those pieces is fixed in cultural memory in a single generally released iteration. The watcher longs to let the young men in the film know what the 'right' words to 'Get Back' are. Yet in that case the footage is long enough ago that at least the hearer does hear a genuine performance, rather than a series of separate parts assembled and doctored within a studio.

bodies in the world now. Perfectly repeating, and technologically enhanced, so that most recorded music bears the same relationship to living human instruments as a VR body does to a real person, the artificial heartbeat of the music industry interposes constant deliberate disruption upon our sense of time, duration and memory.[15] This is a form of worship; and it refuses to acknowledge that time alters human perception, that anything ever needs to change or grow or indeed age or falter. That's a powerful fantasy to be able to sell. The song's artists may become ghosts in their own lives, less real in the culture than their time-frozen images. Many crack under the strain.

Some of music's electronic forms, dance forms, generate intense feeling through a technological formula that has almost nothing to do with our irregular, faulty bodies, as if there might be some reliable mechanized key to a slice of eternity. For example, the song 'It's a Fine Day', which in 1992 became a semi-ambient dance track of exactly this kind, began its life as an unaccompanied, single-voice lyric, a half-private piece of sung domestic memory, set to words by the Manchester poet Edward Barton. Its elusive, recorded moment turned into a highly successful machine for generating reliable electronic joy.[16] The song's history shows starkly the tension between *em*bodied and *un*bodied repetition. It began as something deliberately unprofessional, rough at the edges, framing a little piece of everyday loss. The circular musical form it chose for recording an expressive, dreamlike sadness attracted the attention of a rising industry constructing mass transcendence electronically. (Rave culture was by then a little bit bored with sequencing fragments of Gregorian chant.)[17] In the afterlife of this song's

---

15 The extent to which this is about perfected replications of the past rather than present performance is visible in the remarkably successful Abba concerts using holographic depictions ('digital avatars') of the band's younger selves. See https://abbavoyage.com.

16 Jane and Barton, 'It's a Fine Day' (Cherry Red Records, 1983); Opus III, 'It's a Fine Day' on *Mindfruit* (1992). See https://en.wikipedia.org/wiki/It%27s_a_Fine_Day (accessed 28.2.2023).

17 The German project *Enigma* started that in 1990, with their song

dance music, the joy of it is in the lyrical, fully human fragility of the singing voice heard against the drivingly perfect repetitions of its artificial world. The dance version pushes away the original song's sense of missed chances in favour of an endlessly perfect moment.

Hauntology

If repetition 'denies the ontological character of the new', as Seligman puts it, does that always point reliably 'beyond time'? And if – as I have strongly implied – there is a difference between the worked approximations of a 'live' and effortful iteration (as in minimalism, where the performance of, for example, Steve Reich's *Different Trains*[18] is incredibly hard work for a real ensemble of players) and the perfect effortlessness of electronic replication, what is that difference? It might be that living with the electronic reiterations of a constructed past imposes a kind of stasis upon our experience of living, so that to change or age becomes a kind of reproach, an insult to the perfection of the realler world of electronic memory.

This has a particularly odd twist in it because electronica has in the past been invested with an optimistic futurism, so that its now-historical twentieth-century forms appear to represent limitless promise and yet, being past, are freighted with the weight of a bright future that never arrived. This is what is sometimes called 'hauntology', a word coined by the French

---

'Sadeness (Part 1)', which samples (without permission) the 1976 album *Paschal Mysterium* by the choir Capella Antiqua Munchen for an ambient track which was a huge dance hit, spawning a mass of imitations. The mixture of mourning and sexual reference in the title is neither accidental nor especially considered. See https://en.wikipedia.org/wiki/Sadeness_(Part_I).

18 Steve Reich, *Different Trains* (1988), does use recorded voices but also a live ensemble to think about the trains of World War II, as a Jew, in America and Europe, and the suffering and doomed freight the European trains were carrying.

Marxist-influenced philosopher Jacques Derrida by combining 'haunt' with 'ontology' that also riffs on the first words of the *Communist Manifesto*, 'A spectre is haunting Europe'.[19] Although its coining is in the context of Marxist disappointment with global capitalist dominance, it's also (as is often the case with Derrida) a way of reinventing metaphysics without having to bother with God. As Mark Fisher puts it, 'hauntology [is] ... *the agency of the virtual* ... that which acts without physically existing'. He identifies two forms of it, characterized, in the words of Martin Hägglund, as 'no longer' and 'not yet'.[20] One refers to 'that which is (in actuality no longer, but remains effective as an actuality (the traumatic 'compulsion to repeat', a fatal pattern). The second sense of hauntology refers to that which (in actuality) has not yet happened, but which is already effective in the virtual (an attractor, an anticipation shaping current behaviour).'[21]

No longer, then, is the experience of grief; not yet, a prophetic haunting, an anticipatory vision binding what *is* to what *might be*. It maps very precisely (and not coincidentally) onto the Christian realm of time between the resurrection and the *parousia*, the exact time in which we who are Christian rely upon sacramental iteration to transform the trauma of the past into future hope.[22]

---

19 See China Miéville, *A Spectre, Haunting: on the Communist Manifesto* (Bloomsbury, 2022), p. 188). The writer Richard Littler, who invented the idea of a town trapped in a 1970s time loop, offers an unsettling and very English take on hauntology on BBC Ideas: https://www.bbc.co.uk/ideas/videos/what-is-hauntology-and-why-is-it-all-around-us/p0729knv (accessed 28.2.2023).

20 Quoted from Martin Hägglund, *Radical Atheism: Derrida and the Time of Life* (Stanford University Press, 2008).

21 Mark Fisher, 'The Slow Cancellation of the Future', in *Ghosts of my Life* (Zero Books, 2014).

22 It is not coincidental because Christian philosophical concepts are at the roots of Marxism, but there is also a new, and occasionally mutual recognition, among these two deeply unfashionable forms of envisaging a better world, that within the barren reiterations of consumer culture, where replication owes more to monetization than to rituals of grief or

We know experientially that modern electronic reproduction can trigger both grief and hope (it is, I think, a universal experience to weep at hearing a song that unexpectedly resurrects one's past self) so we cannot assume that its effects are only stasis. 'We are habituated to the "re" of recording being repressed', acknowledges Mark Fisher, as he thinks about the effect of 'materialized memory' on society's longings and mournings. But he points out that it can also *remind* the listener of a forgotten hope, so that, given certain social conditions, the technological replication of past sounds and sights can trigger a vital 'refusal to adjust to what current conditions call 'reality' – even if the cost of that refusal is that you feel like an outcast in your own time.[23] And, depending on the darkness of the times, being an outcast in them is not necessarily a bad thing.

The experience of the couple on the road to Emmaus as they 'stood still, looking sad' and saying to the stranger alongside them 'we had hoped that he was the one', is of people travelling from one to the other of these two modes of Derridean hauntology.[24] They will arrive at a table where their companion will bless and break bread with them – and then, as he gives them the bread and they recognize who he is, will '[vanish] from their sight'.[25]

Jesus' Blood Never Failed Me Yet

Eucharistic worship, iterative as it is, has a complicated and even a suspicious relationship with ecstatic repetition. Some of

hope, something more vital and less capturable might also be haunting Europe, some better Spirit. I am indebted to China Miéville for the grounds of this observation. And while some parts of the Church of England seem enslaved to the crueller spectre of marketization, just as they were once indebted to the power of Kings and Parliaments, that is not the only truth of the Church's daily witness.

23 Fisher, 'Slow Cancellation'.
24 Luke 24.17, 21.
25 Luke 24.31.

that is to do with the twentieth-century history of liturgy (both Anglican and Roman Catholic), because at about the same time as everyone else was getting interested in the transcendent, timeslipping possibilities of ritual loops, churches began to insist upon intellectual and cognitive assent as the grounds of all worship (as in the shift, at Vatican II, from the Latin to the vernacular Mass). At one and the same time, the Churches began to privilege the unpredictable, the unrehearsedly sincere, and the fiercely propositional.

Liturgists were, perhaps rightly, troubled about experiential techniques that make you *feel* stuff whether you want to or not. The uncomfortable, unstable relationship between the grammar of assent and the repetitions of ecstasy has been playing out in Christian worship for centuries, whether we think of John Wesley's discomfort with his ecstatically worshipping early Methodists out in the woods (he was especially worried by the women), or the massive difference between the cresting rush of a repeated evangelical chorus and the tightly controlled use of repetition in the music of Jonathan Dove. Music, handmaid to worship, is also inclined to get *out of hand*. It disrupts our sense of time; it brings personal memory into the present with terrifying immediacy; it acts upon our bodies so that we weep, or are uplifted, or aroused, without us ever quite deciding it. The place of music in worship is inherently unstable, whether in the dominance of worship bands or within the choral tradition. The aural as well the visual history of Christianity is full of clerical fears that people will worship the wrong thing.

Outside the Christian orbit, though, musicians and artists were falling in love with time-games. In 1971, the composer Gavin Bryars left a tape-loop running, in order to transfer the recording he had made of an unnamed tramp singing a fragment of an evangelical hymn, 'Jesus' Blood Never Failed Me Yet'.[26] He came back from his lunchbreak to find the students

---

26 Gavin Bryars, *Jesus' Blood Never Failed Me Yet* (1971) was first performed by *Music Now Ensemble* at the Queen Elizabeth Hall in 1972. It was recorded on Brian Eno's *Obscure* label in 1975.

in his block silent, sombre and tearful, as they constantly re-experienced its shakily mortal affirmation of absolute trust: *'Jesus' blood never failed me yet, never failed me yet. Jesus' blood never failed me yet: there's one thing I know, that he loves me so'*. The fragment ends on an unfinished phrase, so that the ear's impetus to send us back to the beginning stutters a little. In the composer's own words, it 'repeated in a slightly unpredictable way'. Bryars gave it a simple backing of ever-building strings, and it exists at different lengths, running from 25 minutes to one recording of over an hour, made with the singer Tom Waits. In my experience, listening to it banishes the awkward division between devotional and aesthetic experience, and I cannot hear it unmoved – or bear it often. Who the original singer was is not known.

Interrupted Repetition

In contemplating the eucharist in time, we enter into an event that has neither the hope nor the expectation of a perfect replication of a past event. It is not anything like a recording, not a perfect unit that present worshippers receive without being able either to enter or to alter its experience. Instead, the worshippers *are* that experience, and what they receive is a symbolic shape they are invited to inhabit. Without them it cannot *be*, at all.

The eucharist is built on Jesus's command to eat bread and share wine together 'in remembrance of me'. It recollects backwards in its re-instantiating of the single past event of Jesus's actions at the Last Supper, and it does this through imitating his words and actions in stylized form. It also repeats forwards, because it does it again and again. '*As often as* you eat this bread and drink this cup, you proclaim the Lord's death until he comes', writes Paul to the Christians of Corinth, picking up words he ascribes to Jesus: 'Do this, *as often as* you drink.' The words Paul records in his letter he describes as 'received from the Lord' and then 'handed on to you'.[27] Its iterations are as full of change as history itself.

Though this is the earliest of our New Testament documents of witness, it is already in a cycle of repetition, subject not only to the preserving properties of memory, but also to its gaps, its forgettings and distortions. Like all remembering, this is *interrupted* repetition, changing the nature of what it preserves in the act of its preservation. What makes it live is not that Jesus did and said exactly these things at the Last Supper – we trust that he did, but we do not *know*: Paul was not there, and never met Jesus in the flesh. What makes communion live is that in the re-instantiation of his words and actions in the ritual, *Jesus says and does those things now, and here.* 'If there are times past and future, I desire to know where they are', writes St Augustine as he considers the nature of memory. 'But if as yet I do not succeed, I still know, wherever they are, that they are not there as future or past, *but as present.*'[28] Communion sees the past act here and now – present and active, powerful in the living bodies and words and actions of the Body of Christ in our time and place. In what *we* do, and hear, and feel, and speak, and remember.

The Letter to the Hebrews pondered the difference between ritual offerings repeated over and over by flawed mortals, and the sacrifice of himself made once for all by the Son of God. 'Unlike the other high priests', runs its argument, '[Jesus] has no need to offer sacrifices day after day, first for his own sins, and then for those of the people; this he did once for all when he offered himself. For the law appoints as high priests those who are subject to weakness, but the word of the oath, which came later than the law, appoints a Son who has been made perfect for ever.'[29]

---

27 1 Corinthians 11.23–26.

28 Augustine, *Confessions*, 11.18, see https://www.leaderu.com/cyber/books/augconfessions/bk11.html (accessed 14.2.2023). Emphasis mine.

29 Hebrews 7.26–28.

Were this vision of ritual offering to be the whole story, repeated sacramental worship would be redundant. Once, and then never again. But this too is an argument about what God does *not* need, not an argument about what human beings *do* need. Unlike Jesus, we are subsisting in time and space, in the mortal here and now. We need an image, and a means, for how our fleetingness and God's forever come together, or we *will* fall subject to despair.

For that, we need to keep bringing the mess and chaos, the violence and loss of the world as it is, into the ritual space we set up to replicate God's blessed forever. ('*What happened* comes into the house of *what is always happening*, and sits with it together, and eats at its table.') As well as the instantiation of Jesus's presence, both in the act of remembering and in the anticipation of the timeless heaven for which the sip and taste of a token amount of bread and wine represent a brief glimpse, our *own* memories, in all their imperfection and loss and *aporia*, also come to the holy table. This is not just about the memory of Jesus. This is about the memories we bring to remembering Jesus.

Metanoia

The experience of eucharist is not a spectator experience; not something to emerge from unchanged. Each time we go into its process we make ourselves subject to a reversal of mind, a change of heart. Eucharist includes an act of repentance for a reason, but *all throughout* the experience of the eucharistic rite, we are being turned towards a different way of inhabiting life. We are led into what John's Gospel calls 'abiding', or 'dwelling' in the Jesus who we take into ourselves in eucharist.[30]

The long history of arguments about how wide the time-gap should be between personal reiterations of the change-process of eucharist happened because of our differences about *how*

---

30 Cf. John 15.9–11 and passim.

we think eucharist works its change upon us, how deliberately active we think we might need to be in that change. The manuals of devotion common to the centuries before our own concentrated on a long preparatory discipline of realization, demanding much emotional labour; the sign that eucharist had wrought its change was often said to be tears. We break; we melt; we fall if we are to hope to stand. One technical name for the process is the Greek word *metanoia*.

Yet *metanoia*, literally 'mind-change',[31] before it became a technical term for the conversion of the soul, personified the experience of regret and loss. Literally, personified it. *Metanoia* was the shadowy goddess of the missed moment, the darker twin to *Kairos*, god of opportunity. Later, Philo of Alexandria re-purposed *Metanoia* as the attentive handmaid to Christian transformation through the miracle of grace. But much of her make-up, the natural qualities she possesses of sorrow and remorse, send us not towards fulfilment but towards regret: not just for what has passed, but for what never came to be; and not just remembering, but for what memory no longer retains. This too is interrupted repetition, a sense of the loss that time will impose, all that will (and all that will not) happen. The baby who will never see age, the man who will be killed in his prime, the friend who will betray and fall into self-destruction.

O Jesu parvule
Nach dir is mir so weh.

Imitating omnipresence

The theology of the eucharist in time is full of beautiful, satisfying balances and paradoxes, history against eschatology, time against eternity, simple against mysterious, single against repeated, occasional against constant. I could talk about these, and many have; I could talk, for example, about Plato's theory,

---

31 Absolutely literally, something closer to 'change-perceiving'.

in the *Timaeus*, of time as a 'working model' of eternity, a succession of constantly repeating present moments which attempt to make repetition stand for changeless reality, 'like', as C. S. Lewis put it, 'trying to imitate omnipresence by visiting as many places as possible in rapid succession'.[32] The repetitions of eucharist could be seen as that kind of constant rehearsal across time, taking the 'once for all' of Jesus's sacrificial self-offering and making it into a 'working model' of his continual presence. In such a theory of the eucharist in time, our work must be the continual reinsertion of the world's losses, in time and space, into the iterated model in order to bring our mortality together with his divinity.

And, yes, I do think that. I find it a most beguiling and helpfully neat pattern. But *in practice* there is nothing remotely neat about it. The materials themselves, words and bodies, even the flawed human attention itself, are full of slippage. However much we, like the Emperor Constantine, fill the space of our holy ritual with rich adornment, the ground upon which we pile them is still the lost remains of a garden, full of signs and remnants.

Lost Gardens

Within the rite of eucharist, the iteration of the same words, the same actions, across a life of worship, sets up a different structure from the linear for the action of time. Layered into its structure, not horizontally but vertically, going deep and deeper while the top layer, like a repeated note, remains unaltered, is the past, present and active.

Every time I speak the Prayer of Humble Access at the early, Book of Common Prayer, communion service, there rises up before me the dark shine of old wood in an exceptionally beautiful Suffolk church, decades and decades ago. With it also arises a chaotic anguish I never otherwise remember, lost

---

32 Plato, *Timaeus*, 37d, cited by C. S. Lewis in the chapter 'World', in *Studies in Words* (Cambridge University Press, 1960), p. 226.

with the turmoil of that particular bad time, poured into the words 'thou art the same Lord, whose property is always to have mercy'.

Coming towards the end of the acclamation, 'renew us with your Spirit, inspire us with your love, and unite us in the body of your Son', I see the face of the vicar in the church where I discovered worship as a teenager, exhorting his congregation, in a voice just a little too loud, 'Everyone should say these words together! They are for us all!' The mixture of embarrassment and curiosity I felt is preserved in the amber of the words themselves, along with a strong affection. I didn't know then what he was trying to teach us, but I do now. I have lost his name.

A congregation member, whose long-term illness means she can neither come to church nor eat food, watches the livestream of the eucharist her husband is attending. He sits in sight of the camera, an empty seat beside him. On the screen rises the church she has not entered for ten years, populated with a community of which she is a part and which she can never physically join. As the time comes to receive, and she sees her husband take and eat the bread, she visualizes herself beside him, taking and eating. The recollection of Christ's body – wafer, community, intimacy – feeds her as she has never been fed by the home communions she regularly receives. Memory is present now, and here, working for her strength and comfort.

Speaking with people who have received communion over many years, I am struck by how often the beloved dead are present in the circle of those who receive: fathers and husbands, wives and mothers, children and lovers and friends, invoked through the reiterations from past to present, never closer than in the taking of bread and wine.

Meeting to discuss a village funeral, the dead man's daughter says, 'I always think of the words that we say every week, "Lord, I am not worthy that you should come under my roof".' She remembers that the words were said by a centurion, and that the much-loved church in which the funeral will take place has Roman pillars. The connection brings a remembered Jesus into her own place, her own time, and she holds on to that.

I bring communion at home to a beloved parishioner; we have prayed together for years. He is dying. He weeps as he receives. Outside the big glass doors of the room we are in, the grey light shines like water at sundown, and drops of rain tremble on the plants he loves to grow, bright as crystal.

Tragic Interruption

These are undramatic, everyday examples, though also, some of them, examples of grief that is hard to handle. But the iterations of eucharist must take the disjunctive and the violent as well as the ordinary ills the flesh is heir to.

In February 2020, the Revd Jacqui Lewis, an American Presbyterian minister in New York, offered a communion that memorialized Trayvon Martin, the black teenager shot in a random encounter in 2012 whose death, inexplicably, was not treated as murder. As well as (not, to judge from the video, instead of) bread and wine, the congregation shared sweets and watermelon iced tea, the snacks he had bought from the 7–11 store minutes before being shot.[33]

The symbolic overlay of that violent death, a death that should never have happened, with God's *deliberate* sacrifice, makes, in one respect, perfect emotional sense. Like the many ways in which Jesus is brought into the time and place of human suffering, it puts human time and God's time together. Yet Twitter responses included a fair bit of outrage. For some, the alteration of the rite made straightforwardly blasphemous claims. For others, it eliminated the sacred altogether. I don't think those things, and it moves me. But I do think it came too close to making the suffering of Trayvon Martin carry a burden that was properly, and once for all, Jesus's own. Random violence is not redemption. It is destruction. Human beings bring

---

33 https://www.youtube.com/watch?v=YpbwaWEDcCg&t=0s (accessed 14.2.2023).

their sorrows to the foot of the cross, but the person it holds is Jesus.

That particular communion does bring, though, something into view which is otherwise hard to see. 'On the night *that he was betrayed*', begins the re-narration, the re-iteration of the acts of the last supper. We quickly understand from that, that we mark the crisis of a life, the meaning of a life, even perhaps the high point of a life, in the reiteration of eucharist. But our hindsight makes it much harder to see that we are also marking the *tragic interruption* of a life, its shrinking down of choices and possibilities, its vista of ordinary joys, into one grim trajectory. This young, healthy, extraordinary man will be tortured and killed for no good reason. He will be taken away from the web of relationships, of loving and being loved, of doing and being done unto.

In the garden at Gethsemane Jesus mourns the vanishment of futures that will never come to be, that are *ordained* never to be. His disciples will not see any meaning in what happens next, in spite of all Jesus's own efforts to help them see it, because the future they envisaged was full of miraculous meals and liberated glory. It was never – would never be – like that.

Blossoming in the dust

Most deaths do not have clear meanings. The deaths of the young can look most obviously pointless; and even martyrs, as they gamble meaning against continuing to exist, cannot know whether the death they die will blossom in the dust or simply blow away forgotten on the wind. Eucharist does not only hold the *meaning* of death. It brings its *meaninglessness* to the holy table and shows it, with anguish, asking how the loss could ever be given its true worth.

Sometimes the loss is violent. Often it is the everyday shrinking of possibility, the slow death of hope. W. H. Auden's early ballad 'When I walked out one evening' expresses the same gradual emptying of the world:

In headaches and in worry
. Vaguely life leaks away
And Time will have its fancy
Tomorrow or today.[34]

This is the loss of what might have been in the future and now
never will be.

'Jesus, remember me'

During the days of Easter, having laid the table with the bread
and the wine, we make this offertory prayer:

> Be present, be present, Lord Jesus Christ, our risen high priest:
> make yourself known in the breaking of the bread.[35]

Behind the invocation lies the experience of the Emmaus travellers who could not see meaning in Jesus's death, stuck as they
were on the hauntological border between *no longer* and *not
yet*. Though they did not recognize who was walking alongside
them, they said of him later, 'did not our hearts burn within us
while he was talking to us on the road, while he was opening
the scriptures to us?'

Before ever they could name who was speaking, his words
restored a present meaning to the meaningless absence of the
man they mourned. For them, the moment of recognition, the
point where they knew that memory had become present as
a living person – as Jesus – was at the breaking of the bread.
Yet, as they saw what they saw, and knew what they knew, the
present Jesus 'vanished from their sight', leaving only the bread
broken upon the table.

---

34 W. H. Auden, 'As I Walked Out One Evening', in *Collected Poems*,
ed. Edward Mendelson (Faber & Faber, 1976) p. 114.

35 'Prayers at the Preparation of the Table', K2, Easter Season, in
Common Worship: Times and Seasons (Church House Publishing, 2006),
p. 435.

We do not know if they ate the bread he left them. Luke tells us only that 'that same hour' they 'got up and returned to Jerusalem' where they found the eleven apostles saying to each other 'he has risen indeed!' 'Then', says Luke, 'they told what had happened on the road, and how he had been made known to them in the breaking of the bread.'[36]

All over the defaced garden of this world lie the signs and remnants of the Lord's presence, like broken bread on an empty table. Our Lord shows himself in the possibilities we realize in the ritual of eucharist, where the quick promise of what might or could be gives us the impetus to act with hope. He shows himself in the signs and patterns we make, in the schemes of devotion that hold our attention. He shows himself, too, in the fracturing of those same schemes of knowledge, where breaks in perception and argument, like cracks in a pavement, make spaces for green plants to serve our need. He shows himself in the drama of making, in sacred place that invites and eases prayer, in the sacred actions by which we inhabit his holiness. He shows himself in the stuttering repetitions by which we connect our time to his eternity, and he shows himself when we fail to make those connections, or trap ourselves in our own longing for a perfect past. He is not a ghost, not a haunting; he is more than a possibility and larger than a wish. He scatters our lives with gifts of meaning, more than we can count. He brings us home.

I have talked at some length about the many ways that human beings make time serve their sense of meaning – poetry and song, technological reproduction, time-denying repetitions, the copiousness of worldbuilding, all the many ways in which the past is brought into the quick world of now and sent forward into burgeoning possibility. We are makers, no doubt. But we do not make things for ever. Time will have his fancy in the end; and we will be abandoned by our meaning-making, left with snapped handfuls of the threads that once tied our past to our future. And in that time, that last time, all the godlike

---

36 Luke 24.28–35.

actions of humanity fall away, all the possibilities of idolatry abandon our souls, and we are left only with the remembrance God makes of us.

'Jesus,' said the thief beside the dying Christ, 'remember me'.[37] When (as we will) we have nothing left, the body and blood of Jesus will sustain us into Paradise, the garden whose signs and remnants scatter the ground of our strange, flawed, ambiguous, promising world.

And when these failing lips grow dumb
And mind and memory flee,
When Thou shalt in Thy kingdom come,
Jesus, remember me.[38]

---

37 Luke 23.42–43.
38 James Montgomery, 'According to thy Gracious Word', first published in *The Christian Psalmist* (1825).

Printed in Great
Britain
by Amazon